POWER TALK

The Art of Effective Communication

Howard J. Rankin Ph.D

StepWise Press

MA6 1-602

Published by StepWise Press
PO Box 4797
Hilton Head Island, South Carolina
SC 29938-4797

(843) 842 7797

First printing, June, 1999

Library of Congress Catalog Card Number 98-85059
ISBN: 0-9658261-3-9
Printed in the United States

Cover design by ag2 inc., Hilton Head Island, South Carolina

2

TO MJ
JAMES, JOSH and ELLEN

Contents

Acknowledgments

As is typical with a venture of this nature, many people helped to make this book possible.

David Anderson and his team at Anderson Communications and ag2 were, as always, supportive and professional. Special thanks to Robin Wade and Joe Bergeron.

Margaret-Anne Slawson and her colleagues at Access Publishers Network were helpful in the promotion of the book and tolerating some initial delays.

Angela Fugate at McNaughton & Gunn once again did a splendid job of overseeing the printing process.

Extra special thanks go to Kathy and Vern Davidhizar for letting me use their wonderful hideaway location which enabled me to ultimately finish the book. Thanks to their children, Matt, Morgan, Justin and Amanda for tolerating my temporary intrusion into their lives.

My clients always provide me the most insight into the human condition and, in this case, the art of communication and I am eternally grateful to all of them.

Finally, my wife MJ, sons James and Josh as well as my mother-in-law Ellen, were all extraordinarily patient while waiting for me to finish this book. To all of them, my love and heartfelt gratitude.

Introduction

Human beings are not good communicators. Despite the availability of tools and approaches that are known to enhance communication, many of us are unskilled in effective interaction. In many ways, we have barely moved beyond the instinctive communication patterns of lower species.

Good communication means making real contact with another person which is a risky and difficult proposition requiring two abilities. First, you as the communicator need to be able to step outside the boundaries of your own ego and really extend yourself to understand the other person. Second, courage is needed to have the meaningful interaction that ensues when you do extend yourself to another human being.

The ego is the thermal underwear of our psyche. Like thermal underwear, the ego allows our innermost processes to be kept within, keeping us warm, comfortable and protected form the harsh elements of the outside world. Wear thermal underwear that's too tight , however, and you could implode. On the other hand, thermal underwear that has holes in it could leave you suffering from frost bite and over exposure. Wearing the right thermal underwear requires a delicate balance.

The problem with most of our communication is that is given and received with too much thermal underwear. We keep the barriers up, not extending ourselves and not letting the other person in. As a result, most interaction is humdrum, banal and lacking in any real meaning. When was the last time you had a meaningful conversation with someone other than your therapist?[1]

---

[1] If you're not having meaningful conversation with your therapist, find another one fast.

There is a serious downside to this communication deficit. If meaningful communication is hard to find, so is meaning. Hardly surprising then, that there is currently a tremendous thirst for meaning and a re-evaluation of values in America today.

There is a misconception that there is no meaning in people's lives today. This is nonsense. There just is not meaningful communication.

Meaning comes frrm sharing experiences. Without such sharing we are reduced to a ramshackle collection of individuals each trying to comprehend our own experience in the vacuum of our own thermal underwear. People do have significant lives - they just don't talk about them. Without such communication, some real contact, we don't hear ourselves talk about our meaning, we never get a chance to articulate it, understand it, share it. It remains trapped within.

Ironically, in the technological society where communications predominate, communication deteriorates. The average parent spends 38 minutes per week in meaningful conversation with his or her child and three hours and forty-five minutes per day watching television.

It is true that communications are becoming more interactive. Visit any chat room on the internet, however and amid the anonymous profanity and disembodied nonsense you will surely conclude that such interactivity is a mixed blessing.

It is tempting to conclude, of course, that the people who hide behind the anonymity of their screen names spouting profanity are the dregs of society, the angry aberrations that are beyond redemption.

Here is a recent conversation I had in a chat room.

Me: Can I have a meaningful conversation in here?

X: F---- off!

Me: Seriously, does anyone want to really chat?

X: F---- off you s---bag!

Me: I'd like a one-on-one conversation of substance

X: Okay, let's have a one-on-one, a------!

Me: Okay let's IM

This conversation has not started on a very promising note. It looks as if it is going nowhere positive. But wait!

X: What's your problem, a------!

Me: My problem is that no-one wants to have a serious conversation.

X: Why do you want to have a serious conversation, you a------?

Me: I find them rewarding, don't you?

X: Don't know. Not sure I've ever had one.

Me: Well, you could try. I'd like to have one with you.

X: (after some delay) I'm sorry about all that cussing

Me: That's okay. You're probably frustrated that no-one talks to you

X: That's right, I suppose

Me: You're not exactly inviting that are you?

X: There are too many bull------- out there!

Me: True!

X: Are you a bulls------?

Me: Not now

We then proceeded to have a long, meaningful conversation about this young man's hopes and frustrations. For about an hour, he had adjusted his thermal underwear.

Communication is a spiritual issue. It is spiritual not just in the fact it requires personal extension and understanding but that it is a prerequisite for articulating the meaning in our lives.

Communication skills are therefore the most valuable personal resource. Despite huge technological advances, or even because of them, the need to communicate effectively and influentially has never been greater. In business and in personal life, effective communication is a prerequisite for success. Communication is the road down which every other aspect of life has to travel. Pot-holed, ill maintained roads create bumpy and hazardous rides. Well surfaced highways allow for smooth, comfortable journeys.

For those who were not blessed, either by genetics or exposure, with natural communication skills, there is hope. While communication may not come easily, techniques that improve personal effectiveness and power can be learned. Following a few simple rules and adapting communication accordingly can make a dramatic difference to your life. You have to be willing, however, to act with grace, humility and patience.

The techniques described in this book are tools. All tools can be used productively or malevolently. A hammer can be used to construct a beautiful building or as a murder weapon. It is my fervent hope that the techniques described will be used in a constructive way enabling people to reach out and foster sharing. The fact is, however, that the same principles that can help save someone's life can also be used by a confidence trickster to swindle an old lady. It's not the principle's fault.

I thought long and hard about calling this book 'Empowering Talk' because I hope that the book will empower its readers. Good communication is also motivation and thus empowering. In the end, because the approaches and principles described in this book are powerful, I opted for 'Power Talk.' In any event, it is meant to be a practical book describing the techniques that constitute the art of effective communication.

The study and development of the described techniques were fueled in many cases by the profit motive. That does not make them any less valuable. There can be a reflexive distrust of business because of its natural preoccupation with the bottom line. Good business, however, is good personal relations. In the final analysis, business is about individuals and their interactions. Those companies that recognize and strive honestly for that, will survive and thrive.

Business has pioneered the art of strategic communications, even if many businesses do not take advantage of this knowledge. Corporations do not have to be the sole proprietor of strategic communications, however. Strategic communication at a personal level can and does lead to both greater personal influence and more effective relationships.

I have spent most of my career as a clinical psychologist and therapist. If I had been asked in the early part of my career what I was trying to achieve in therapy I would have replied that I was applying known techniques for specific problems. Subsequently, I came to realize that over and above the application of proven techniques, I was really in the communication and influence business.

It initially shocked me to realize that I shared my craft with salespeople, negotiators and marketers. Healing people and selling them things do not initially appear to be the same endeavor. In some ways, of course, they are not, but at the fundamental level they do share one key element in common - they both try to get people to take action. Trying to motivate and exert influence is part of everybody's life – both professional and personal.

With the realization that my job heavily depended on my ability to communicate and influence, I set out to learn all I could about the subject. The result of my efforts form the basis of this book.

My own experience has shown me that most people are egocentric in their communication. We make our point, express our feelings, pitch our proposal without often stopping to really consider our audience. We want to express ourselves, which is fine, but often that is not the way to find mutual consent and to get what we want. Moreover, we do not approach achieving our goals in a very organized or logical way. We make few attempts to understand our listener and devise strategies that take them, their perceptions and sensitivities into account in our communication strategies.

Most of us also mistakenly believe that communication is about logic. Effective communication and influence are not primarily about logic or common sense, -- they are about emotion and experience. A central theme to this book is that effective communication is about creating the right experience and eliciting the right emotions. The experience is the message.

Human beings are programmed to make sense of the world around them. Uncertainty is far too unsettling for the human mind and we will go to great lengths to construct explanations, even if they are detrimental to us, rather than put up with the unknown. We have to have meaning and are constantly creating a framework of interpretation that allows us to understand, and ultimately control, our environment.

We are thus programmed to tell ourselves stories for the sake of our sanity. Understanding the story-telling process and how the listener constructs his or her stories is fundamental to effective communication. Communication is story-telling. The work on

14

story-telling has been one important strand of knowledge that has influenced my thinking about this subject.

There have been two other strands of work in the influence field that have had a significant impact on my thinking and behavior.

The first is from the work of a psychotherapist called Milton Erickson. Erickson was arguably the greatest practitioner of psychotherapy. He had an intuitive understanding of how to influence people, especially his clients. His techniques for overcoming resistance, the use of metaphor, hypnotic language patterns and a host of other techniques have had a profound impact on the helping professions and beyond. Ericksonian Psychotherapy is based on his insights and practice and the Milton Erickson Foundation, based in Phoenix, is a testament to his continued influence in the counseling world.

The other area of thinking and practice that has influenced me has been the work of social psychologists who have researched and articulated fundamental human processes that underpin the art of communication and influence. Of these social psychologists the work and writings of Robert Cialdini have been especially insightful and enlightening. Cialdini's classic and scholarly book, Influence: Science and Practice is highly recommended for those who want more scientific detail of the fundamental social psychological processes in the art of influence presented in a highly readable form.

I have used examples form all walks of life to show the true universality of the principles and techniques described. Like personal communication, business communication only works if it makes real contact with its audience, whether that audience consists of employees, fellow managers or customers. I have tried to use business examples because I believe that business has a huge influence in our culture. It determines our daily lives in so many ways that a more communication-oriented and sensitive business community would benefit all of us. In addition, a business that makes real contact with its employees and consumers will be a successful business.

I hope that this book influences you to consider, and where necessary improve, your own communication skills. To this end, I have challenged the reader throughout the book to consider how the described principles can be applied in his or her own setting, whether that is corporate or any other aspect of life.

Howard J. Rankin Ph.D
May 1999

Chapter 1

The Experience Is The Message
It's not what you say, it's the way that you say it.

One purpose of communication is to share reality. You may want customers to view you as the market leader, your boss to appreciate your efforts or your spouse to know that you are mad. In all of these examples, you are trying to get your target audience to see the world as you see it.

Whether your goal will be achieved will depend on two things: The listener's experience and your communication skills. One thing is certain in this interaction. Your persuasiveness will have less to do with logic and more to do with how well you can create the right experience. That experience is created by the *total interaction* you share with the listener.

The essence of communication is the subtext, the experience, not just or even the words or information that are conveyed. A subtitle for this book could be "The Experience is the Message."

Human beings have evolved over millions of years and language and logic are relatively new developments. It is the older, primitive, Reptilian brain that controls much of our behavior. In this older brain, experience is stored and emotions and primitive instincts are activated. These are powerful forces that can and do overwhelm logic and drive our behavior, often unconsciously. The plain fact of the matter is that, for human beings, experience is king.

If logic were able to consistently overwhelm the primitive brain it would be easy to simply talk people out of destructive behavior, bad habits and poor choices. Twenty-five years in counseling has shown me, however, that few people, if any, can be talked out of behavior they want to change, let alone behavior they do not want to change. The realization that argument and appeals to logic rarely work was what led me to consider what did work. That in turn led me to techniques of influence, communication and ultimately to this book.

There is no objective reality. Events are seen through our individual filters, flawed and colored by our unique experience. Consequently, the same event can have as many different meanings as there are observers. Each of us creates our own reality from our experiences and these are based on our perceptions.

Later in this book, I will go into more detail about the nature of our interpretative capacities. For now, it is suffice to say that as a matter of survival we need to make instant judgments about what is happening in our environment. We thus have developed shortcuts to help manage the environment and survive. Unfortunately, those shortcuts, while necessary, can sometimes lead us astray. For example, once we have perceived an event or a person in a certain way it is difficult to change that impression and it is impossible to wipe out the experience. That is why so much store is put on first impressions. Perception is reality.

It will be no surprise to learn, therefore, that much of this book is devoted to what is known about how to create the right experience. Creating the right experience to maximize influence involves knowing what tools to use both in trying to understand the audience and in guiding communication. Communication is always taking place even when you are not consciously involved in interaction.

Subtext Communication In Practice
Not too long ago, I run into a problem with my computer. After experiencing the frustration of trying to reach technical support, I was eventually told by a recorded message that I could e-

mail the technical support department, which I duly did. There was an almost instant reply message acknowledging my problem and assuring me that someone would get on the problem right away.

Days passed. I e-mailed again. More days passed. I e-mailed again and eventually, nearly a month after my original SOS, I got a reply and some help with my problem. A few days later, Customer Support e-mailed asking me to comment on the service I received. Well, I was not too impressed with the service I had received. In fact, I was downright irritated that it has taken the best part of a month for anyone to offer a constructive solution. So I wrote to customer service telling them that I was not too impressed and their company was on the verge of losing a loyal customer.

To this day (more than a year and a half later so it is safe to assume I'm not getting a reply) I have not had a reply from customer service and needless to say I no longer do business with the company. Ignoring me was about the worst thing they could have done. All their lack of courtesy meant to me was here was a company that does not care. Even customer service, which is meant to rectify the operational problems that customers will inevitably experience, did not care!

As luck would have it, another part of my electronic equipment, an LCD projector, also run afoul of gremlins at about the same time. I was just as irritated with that as I was with my computer problems because the LCD projector should not have had those problems and, even more galling, the warranty had just expired! I was furious. I wanted them to carry all the costs of the repairs.

When I called customer service at the LCD company, however, they handled me expertly. They were understanding. They validated my feelings. They explained their situation and made a rational proposal about what they would do for me. We negotiated a reduced rate for the repairs but that really was not the point. *They made me feel as if I was dealing with rational people who were treating me fairly.* They may not have been treating me fairly. For all I know I may have paid through the nose for a simple

19

repair. They guided me to a place where I was willing to see them as a reasonable company worth doing business with. Note, they could have ripped me off royally, but as long as they guided me to feel positive about them, they had won me over. Customer service is not about capitulating to the customer's demands but guiding the customer to feel positively about the company. Making the public feel positively towards the company is a critical function of every corporate employee and representative.

Perception is Reality

If a customer perceives the world's best service company as offering bad service, then the customer's reality is that they are bad at service. Communication (in every aspect, from advertising, to the personal behavior of the lowest person in the organization) should be designed to lead the client to a positive perception of the organization even when mistakes have been made and disagreements arisen.

Many corporations, in fact a majority of them, fail to appreciate this crucial aspect of customer relations. They will spend a fortune on advertising and public relations but pay little attention to standard letters that go to customers and potential clients.

For example, one HMO routinely sent out letters to their subscribers that were cold and impersonal. I am sure that this is typical for the industry, indeed most industries. Yet impersonal and cold communications seem even more inappropriate for companies that make their money brokering their clients' well-being.

Here is a letter that was routinely sent, no doubt typical of the genre for HMO's in general. The originals had the bracketed data fields duly filled.

"Dear

The Health Services Department of XYZ™, Inc. XYZ™ has received information from (Physician/hospital) regarding your (procedure) on (date). Based on review of this information, XYZ™ will not provide coverage for the admission after 11:59 pm on (date) with an expected discharge of (date). The medical information does not support the need for continued acute inpatient care.

Any decision to continue services without authorization remains with you and your physician. Based on your Certificate of Coverage/Summary Plan Description benefits may be provided, if medically indicated, in either a skilled facility or your home with prior authorization by your physician.

If you do not agree with this decision you have the right to appeal. You may initiate the appeal process by contacting Customer Service at this address or by calling 1-999-999-9999. For more information, the procedure for members appeals is outlined in the Certificate of Coverage/Summary Plan Description. If you need a copy of these plans, please contact Customer Service.

If you have any questions, please contact Customer Service Department at 1-999-999-9999.

Sincerely,"

Imagine receiving a letter like that. What would your reaction be? I know mine would be one of anger and resentment. The focus of the letter is on the negative. What will not be paid. What is not covered. While factually true, that letter is completely patronizing. Such a formal business letter might be appropriate for a fairly hostile business to business communication but as a letter to paying customer it is inappropriate. If indeed communication is more about the sub-message implied in its tone than the facts contained within the message, this letter is at best patronizing and at worst insulting.

So what happens if time is taken, at minimal expense, to change the letter to the following (with the changes emboldened for better understanding).

"Dear

We have received information from (Physician/hospital) regarding your (procedure) on (date). **Fortunately,** this information shows that acute inpatient care will not be necessary following your (procedure). Your group health plan will, therefore, provide coverage for this admission from (date) until 11:59 pm on (date). We expect you to be discharged no later than (date)

If you **choose to have some post-operative** care outside the allowable guidelines **you have the following options:**

- Seek health plan coverage for care in either a skilled facility or your home. Your physicians must get approval from us before such coverage is allowed.

- Continue inpatient care without health plan coverage

If you wish to exercise your right of appeal you can do so by calling one of out Customer Service **team** at 1-999-999-9999 or by writing to us at this address. If you have other questions or want a copy of the guidelines that are in your Certificate of Coverage/Summary Plan description our Customer Service team will be **happy** to assist you.

We wish you well and hope you have a successful and speedy recovery from your (procedure).

Yours sincerely,"

Now, what is your emotional response to this letter? The facts are still the same – you are being informed that charges will not be covered. You might be disappointed that some of your expenses are no going to be reimbursed but you surely will be more accepting and understanding of the decision.

Without venturing too far into a course in business letter writing[2] let us briefly consider the rationale for the changes to the letter.

First, taking out the impersonal corporate trademarked name (which is on the letterhead anyway) and replacing it with a simple "we" makes the letter both more succinct and personal.

Focusing on the positive by emphasizing the anticipated speed of the recovery is naturally more uplifting. Anytime you can use a positive word or phrase, just do it.

The revised letter also spells out the options available to the client in a clear and non threatening, non adversarial way. The revised letter validates the client's rights and choices.

You will also note that the revised version, while recognizing the client's right of appeal, dispenses with the phrase "If you should disagree with the decision.." Describing an action, like disagreeing with a decision, will make visualization of that action much more likely. Visualizing an action often leads to experiencing it as if it were indeed happening. By leading someone to visualize an action, therefore, you are eliciting the experience. It is for precisely that reason that you do not want to give people the opportunity to experience the negative. There is a danger that it will become a self-fulfilling prophecy. As is addressed in the final chapter *this applies as much to self-talk as it does to conversations with others.*

Words have emotional associations which work at the unconscious level. For this reason the revision replaces the word

---

[2] The Master Communicators Institute will help you with that if you wish. Details are given in the back of the book

"staff" with the word "team." The word "staff" sounds like "staph" which is an infection. The word "team" connotes mutual support, togetherness and friendship. Do you want your customer service department to sound like an infection or a colleague?

The revision also takes the opportunity to introduce another positive word. The customer service team are now "happy" to assist clients. Again, this creates an impression of smiling, friendly representatives chaffing at the bit to service the client's every need.

Finally, the revised version rectifies a glaring omission from the original letter. It simply extends wishes to the client that their procedure goes well and that they experience a speedy recovery. This should be a genuine wish. After all, what HMO does not want healthy subscribers?

The revisions are neither difficult to make nor require advanced communication skills. They do require an ability to understand how letters will be received and how to communicate necessary information in a way that creates the most appropriate and favorable experience.

Common sense dictates that the more customers are alienated, the more complaints they will make and the more likely that they will be lost to the competition. A customer receiving the cold, harsh letter described initially may not complain about *that* letter but their anger and resentment at being patronized will be stored and likely resurface at a later date over another issue.

The culture has changed enormously and rapidly in the past four decades. There was a time when the official, even officious, language of a business letter was respected. This was a time when there was a greater respect for authority, large corporations and big business. Today, this respect has eroded and we live in a society where individuals are no longer intimidated by assumed authority and expect to be treated with reverence and respect. Personal service is what is expected with the emphasis on the personal.

Stuffy, formal letters to paying customers just will not cut it any more.

Moreover, traditional business writing once assumed a man-to-man communication that is no longer appropriate when women constitute a sizable part of the workforce and a majority of the buying public. A formal, down to basics, informational letter might be okay for a left brain problem solving man but it is definitely not okay with a more sensitive woman, who is just as good at problem solving but responds more experientially.

This HMO could, for a fraction of the cost of the overall promotion budget, ensure that their communications send the right message and establish the right emotional response in their subscribers. If they trained their entire organization properly in how to respond to customers they could probably end up saving money in their overall promotion budget while considerably enhancing their image and sales. They would also make their subscribers feel more valued.

> **Every syllable uttered by any representative of an organization creates an emotional response and contributes to the company's image**

Communication influences all aspects of personal and corporate life -- management, training, public relations, sales, marketing and customer service. In all of these endeavors the corporation's effective functioning depends on its employees ability to communicate.

Herein lies a major point about this book. Effective communication is about *influence and motivation* rather than control. You can not make people act against their will unless you have some physical control over them. So this is not about force. It is about guiding people to a position where they might embrace your viewpoint and action plan. It is about getting the audience to *own* your idea.

Most of us want as much control as possible. One of the most frustrating things in life is the fact that other people do not act in accordance with our wishes. This can be a major problem in a business setting where performance depends on the actions of subordinates and teammates. In personal life, too, while total control is neither possible nor desirable, some is necessary for psychological survival. Lack of control is the toxic component of negative stress.

Despite this need for influence, however, few are very good at achieving it. Most have a very naïve view of communication and are either ignorant or ignore some of the fundamental tenets of influence.

Egocentric communication is the norm. Communication occurs from an emotional, ego-driven perspective rather than a logical, strategic one. When someone disagrees with us, we get angry or defensive and are likely to become punitive or aggressive. Few of us consider what we need to do <u>strategically</u> to get our way - we just blunder on or drop out.

Not that every message should always be delivered in a very premeditated or unemotional manner – far from it. Being clear headed enough to consider how to reach the listener, however, requires the ability to take a logical rather than an emotional perspective.

The key to effective communication is to get the listener to relate experientially to the message. It is difficult, if not impossible, to stimulate action without eliciting emotion. One of the predominant themes in this book is that effective messages and effective communicators arouse emotions. Stimulating action by appeals to emotion is not a manipulative ploy – it is a genuine, reasonable and necessary way of making the listener understand the real meaning of the message.

Although the idea that effective communication is based on emotion is not new, it is often overlooked and rarely used creatively.

26

For example, I was recently consulting with a local hospital. The administration were trying very unsuccessfully to get people to recycle various materials. The administrator of this particular project was lamenting the fact that the hospital employees just could not or would not grasp the concept of waste. It appeared to me that the hospital staff had no emotional connection at all to the concept of deprivation. If they could not relate to deprivation how could they relate to the notion of recycling which is, after all, about preservation in order to avoid deprivation?

I suggested to the administrator of the project that the only way his project was going to succeed was if the team members responsible for recycling *experienced* deprivation. Until they experienced deprivation, recycling was just another concept and a nuisance concocted by bureaucrats.

Following my suggestion, the administrator organized a system where each administrative department would experience some deprivation for a long enough period to be an inconvenience but not so long as to disrupt productivity. When this department needed more paper, none was forthcoming. When that department needed more envelopes, none was forthcoming and so on until each department had suffered some minor irritation and deprivation. Having experienced minor deprivation the various departments were now more receptive to the recycling idea that was now presented as a way to avoid not just waste but deprivation. As you will learn in this book, fear of loss is a powerful and universal motivator.

Appealing to the listener's experience so that he or she can really understand and empathize with your message is described more in chapter 5. Even when the communication takes the form of skills training rather than motivation, egocentric communication predominates. One amusing example occurs in the wonderful movie "The Full Monty." Gerald, the delegated dance instructor, is having tremendous difficulty communicating the dance steps to his charges. Suddenly one of these charges, Horse, makes a telling experiential connection. He announces with insight, "Oh, this is just like the Arsenal off-side trap,". (This is a well-known tactic of a famous British soccer team known to the dancers in training). With that everyone instantly understands what they have to do, berating Gerald for his poor instruction with the comment "Why didn't you just say that in the first place?"

Gerald did not say that in the first place because he was communicating egocentrically, i.e. without thinking about his audience's frame of reference.

My education was characterized by receiving instruction form "teachers" who showed no interest or aptitude in presenting their material from anything other than their own viewpoint. So when I was hired to teach psychology to medical students at the University of London, I decided that while the material presented would be my choice, the context of the material would be determined by the students. So instead of having to sit through 8 am classes on subjects like psychophysics and animal behavior, the students now visited a hospice to learn about death and dying, had a debate on medical ethics and philosophy and a project on addiction, all contexts in which a majority of them were interested.

Reaching Out
There are various ways of accessing the emotions of your audience. The obvious way is to discover who they are and what makes them tick by listening. Listening carefully will provide many clues about emotions, experiences and symbols. Such clues are not only necessary but vital in the construction and delivery of an motivational message. It is for this reason that listening skills are essential tools in the communicators workbench.

Although listening is the most significant way of uncovering critical personal information, observation is just as important. The way a person dresses, the photos he or she display, the car he or she drives, even the way he or she eats are all potential clues about a person's psyche that are extremely valuable to the good communicator. Such listening is not just about increasing influence. It is about making real contact and getting to know another human being.

It is a human characteristic to seek meaning in all the events we experience. Unless we suffer from certain sorts of brain damage, this process of interpretation is automatic. Each of us interpret our environment a little differently, our perceptions colored and shaped by individual history. Knowing the biases in your perception is a critical communication skill. Effective life management and communication require this self knowledge. Without it, the escape from your own biases into another person's world will not be possible.

Chapter 2

Egocentric Communication
How can there possibly be a different point of view?

Human beings are social animals who depend on each other for survival. There has to be at least a primitive level of communication for any species to survive. Insects have primitive, instinctual communication capacities while mammals have sophisticated ways of interacting and have the capacity to follow linguistic rules.

Even the most primitive communication patterns, while instinctive, do allow for some individual variation, adaptation and modification. These instinctive patterns, for example mating patterns, consist of stereotyped movements from the initiator that elicit behaviors from another member of the species which in turn trigger other behaviors from the initiator. This communication "dance" consists therefore of matching body movements. Symmetry of movement in particular and synchronization in general, are key features of establishing rapport and developing the basis of good communication and influence in human beings as well as the birds and the bees.

These deep seated primitive communication devices influence human communication mare than is imagined. When we think of communication, we think primarily of language yet it is common experience to "read between the lines" of a message or to realize that "actions speak louder than words." Inherently, we recognize the limitations of language.

Language is a fairly recent development from an evolutionary point of view. As a rule, the most recently developed human characteristics are also the ones that can be pre-empted by older and more entrenched ones, especially at critical times. So when the chips are down, actions do speak louder than words and are significant in shaping interpretations of the message.

Managing Automatic Reactions

The theory of evolution predicts that the problem with human beings is that they started out as reactive, instinctive and emotional animals but have evolved to a higher consciousness. The average human is thus daily confronted with a battle between his or her older, instinctive emotions and newer consciousness and reason.

Nowhere is this battle more evident than when communicating. A colleague makes a mistake that has consequences to you. Your first reaction is one of anger. Because you are oblivious of the need to curtail your anger or because of inability to do so, you yell angrily at your co-worker. All this achieves is to arouse reciprocal anger in your colleague. If you have de facto authority over them (e.g. you are their boss) the context may prohibit them from expressing it openly right there and then but they are angry and sooner or later their anger is likely to be used against you. Moreover, not only has your anger achieved a negative outcome it has done nothing to resolve the problem of the mistake.

It is often appropriate to express anger, a natural, primitive response. The purpose of an outburst as described above is to vent and make known your feelings.

If you want to be an effective communicator, however, you cannot continually be acting automatically and allowing primitive responses to take over. A more considered approach is needed. If you want to actually do something about the situation, expressing anger has limited value. A different approach is needed to improve the situation. The right communication strategy will show that....

- You can teach someone how to avoid making mistakes without resorting to anger.

- You can get people to rectify their mistakes without resorting to anger.

- You can even convey anger without yelling.

Moreover, if you try to combine teaching with anger, you will be creating the wrong experience and one that is certainly not conducive to learning.

In Junior High School I was lousy at Science. For some reason I was having a tough time learning the significance of the periodic table of elements. I distinctly remember the chemistry teacher singling me out and screaming some instructions at me. Needless to say, my mind was completely absorbed with dealing with his anger. I could not concentrate on anything else, let alone chemical elements. At that moment, I would not have been able to distinguish a hydrogen atom from the bubble gum that was stuck under the lab bench.

My experience was one of humiliation, anxiety and failure. Hardly surprising then that I was turned off chemistry in particular and science in general, for several years. It was only when I came to these subjects on my own terms some years later, that I developed an interest and aptitude for them.

All of us can relate to the example in the science lab. An account of that interaction in terms of what was being said and what was being heard from the different perspectives looks like this.

Chemistry teacher (says): Rankin, This is simple! The Hydrogen atom is here on this chart! It has a valency of one! Here is the oxygen atom! It has a valency of two!

Rankin (hears and feels): Idiot! Failure! Fool! Embarrassment! Shame! Humiliation!

The example   highlights the relative unimportance of language in some interactions. Although language is phenomenally powerful, it is just one communication tool.

We often forget that everything else about us also is contributing to our message, often in subtle but critical ways. It is the total interaction that counts. Communication is wholistic.

Purpose and Expression

There are two broad categories of communication.

Expressive communication entails the simple expression of thoughts and feelings. It is not primarily designed to provoke a response or to influence others. It is meant to be a statement of some aspect of our personal experience.

Expressive communication does have value. By talking out loud, feelings and thoughts come into sharper focus. The act of expressing feelings helps define exactly what those feelings are. This is one of the great benefits of keeping a journal. Expressing is thinking.

The Yelling Coach

Many years ago, I was part of a team of psychologists researching social interaction between the staff and players of a leading professional soccer team. It was the habit of one of the coaches to sit on the bench yelling profane criticism at the players in an effort to motivate them. When the data was analyzed it was found that the main effect of these supposedly motivational tirades was that all the players avoided that part of the field that was in earshot of the coach!

The expression of feelings can also help relieve the pent-up tension and internalized pressure that accompanies strong emotions. Venting has great therapeutic value.

There is also something else that is important about expressive communication – it is easier and more natural. Most

34

people like to talk about themselves -- a subject that is endlessly interesting and requires little effort. Expressive communication does not require consideration of anyone else. Expressive communication is egocentric communication.

Purposeful communication, on the other hand, is designed to motivate and influence others, whether that is to buy products, accept proposals or improve performance.

There are several problems, however, with purposeful communication.

First, because it is simply not an egocentric expression of our selves, it requires more effort. For one thing, effective purposeful communication means listening to the audience and tailoring your message to their needs.

Second, many people are often very unclear that they have a specific purpose in communicating.

Third, most of us are never trained in how to communicate purposefully. How many courses have you taken in listening skills, non-verbal communication, establishing rapport and techniques of influence? If you have taken even one of these you have done more than the vast majority of the population.

Lack of training in purposeful communication leads to a reliance on expressive communication even when it is not appropriate. As children we have a naturally expressive rather than purposeful style. If you are never trained in anything different, however, expressive and egocentric style will predominate.

The biggest communication mistake most people make, therefore, is that they use expressive and thus egocentric communication even when they are trying to motivate and influence others. This leads to miscommunication, frustration and failure.

As if this was not bad enough, many of us are unclear about the exact purpose of our communication. So we are not sure what it is we are trying to achieve and we are not using the right tools to reach goals we have not articulated!

The use of expressive communication to motivate and influence others is often accompanied by what can be best described as "magical thinking." Magical thinking leads to the conviction that influence is possible when the only grounds for believing this is the fervent desire for it to be so. In my counseling work, I continually comes across individuals who have unrealistic expectations about their ability to change others in their lives. One of the great frustrations in life is the recognition that we cannot control another person unless they are compliant.

Simple expression of feelings and thoughts rarely influence others. Your reality is your reality and it is often not shared by others. We imagine others will immediately empathize with our expressive communication but that rarely happens or is powerful enough to exert real influence. Purposeful communication requires building a bridge between speaker and listener so that their worlds can be connected. Without that bridge, speaker and listener are separate unconnected entities.

Often the communication goals do not conveniently fall into one of these two categories. Communication can sometimes be both expressive and purposeful. So we "share" with the listener specific facts in a certain emotional tone in order to get them to act in a certain way.

Purposeful communication requires the following.

- A clear understanding of what the goals of communication are

- A strategic approach to achieving those goals. Which tools and techniques will be used?

A strategic approach to purposeful communication in which specific strategy and communication devices are used may sound a lot like manipulation.

Manipulation or Motivation?

"Manipulation" is what psychologists call a fat word -- it means different things to different people. In common usage, the word has derived a derogatory meaning to imply scheming for one's own ends.

In my graduate school training in clinical psychology, I was privileged to be serving as an intern to Dr Monty Shapiro, a man widely regarded as the father of British clinical psychology. In one of the ward rounds I attended, the nurses were complaining about a particular patient with panic disorder who was constantly badgering them for more medication to alleviate her high levels of anxiety. The patient was apparently trying all manner of arguments to secure the extra medication. "She's so *manipulative*," the nurses said.

"Why do you say she is manipulative?" Dr Shapiro asked. "If you had extreme panic wouldn't you do everything you could for relief?"

The nurses agreed and ultimately concurred that the patient's behavior was a reflection of her need rather than a personality trait. The word "manipulative" implies the use of games and deceit, to achieve an end. While we are all manipulative and strive for as much control as possible, chronic manipulators use **deceptive practices** to achieve their goals.

The techniques described in this book are meant to be used with integrity and do not depend on deception. The concepts outlined here are designed to utilize what is known about human behavior to deliver an effective message that guides and motivates the listener. They are not designed to trick the listener nor make them act in a way that is detrimental to their interests. If I use communication tactics to influence an alcoholic whose liver is about to fall out to quit drinking, I think I am being motivating rather than manipulative

In general, it is difficult if not impossible to get people to act in a way that is detrimental to them *if you do not resort to deception.* This applies to communication techniques such as hypnosis and other persuasive techniques. You might be able to get people to say the things you want them to say, but not to believe them.

Taking a strategic approach and logically applying proven techniques to maximize influence is not manipulative in the derogatory sense of the word - it is smart.

Purposeful communication is practiced by groups who have learned the secrets to effective communication and influence. Companies spend a vast amount of money on listening (conducting focus groups), understanding their listener's characteristics (market research) and training (skills learning) because it works and is a logical approach. If these companies did not adopt such good communication practices their shareholders would be up in arms. If it is good enough for a Fortune 500 company, it should be good enough for us on a personal level.

Communication Goals

Knowing the purpose of the message is a fundamental part of effective communication. The problem is that much of our communication is habitual and expressive by nature. Frequently, communication goals are poorly articulated.

Even when communication goals are known, there is little consideration of how to structure and deliver the message effectively. This is often the case with confrontations. Frustrated by our listener's inability to do what we want them to do, we apply even more pressure in the form of louder and louder talk and more and more threats. Most of the time this alienates the listener making it less and less likely that the goal of securing his or her compliance will be achieved.

In essence, what we all want is control. We want as much control of our lives simply because anything less becomes threatening. Lack of control is stressful which is why losses (e.g death of a loved one, divorce) are frequently rated the most stressful life-events. Most of these events are irreversible and emphasize our lack of control.

> *The purpose of communication is to gain control of our environment*

A Strategy For Purposeful Communication

The rest of this book is about the tools that will enhance influence by establishing real contact with the audience. Here are some key questions to begin with

- **What am I trying to achieve with this communication?**

This can be easily answered by finishing the following statement.

"The outcomes I am trying to get by this communication are..."

Those outcomes could be anything. You might want a hug, recognition or a client's signature. If there is more than one desired outcome, prioritize.

Let's proceed through these steps on the assumption that you are asking for a raise. This is a good example because most people do not take a strategic approach to this request. Instead they "feel" as if they deserve a raise and simply express that opinion. In short, they use expressive, egocentric communication when purposeful strategies are required.

- **How will the listener/audience react to your desired outcome?**

Is your boss willing to give you a raise? What, if anything will he or she want in return? How close are you to agreement?

If you are miles apart, what, if anything **can** you agree on? For example, does your boss agree that you deserve a raise (even if his budget doesn't allow for it)? If your boss doesn't agree that a raise is merited, does he or she at least agree that you are competent and do good work?

- **Why will your message be resisted?**

Will your raise request be resisted because ...

a) There's no extra money to fund it
b) Your boss doesn't value you
c) It's not the right time
d) Other considerations

Of course, you will not always know how your listener is going to react, in which case you have to plan a response to each of several possible replies.

- **What do I know about the listener/ audience that will help me tailor my message for maximal influence?**

Suppose your boss is a little paranoid and does not take well to perceived threats. Charging into his office screaming, "If you don't give me a raise I'm going to immediately join your competitors!" is not a high probability tactic. It might make you feel good but it is unlikely to make your boss feel good and thus doomed to failure. Even if you did get a raise under these circumstances, chances are that in most cases[3] it would come back to haunt you later when the superior is in a less intimidated position, i.e. when he or she has lined up your replacement.

If the experience is the message, it will be important for the boss to feel good about complying with your request. Ideally, you want your boss to *own* the idea of a raise.

You could, for example, ask for a review of your prospects which would provide insight into the boss's thinking about your future within the organization.

Rather than approach the subject directly, a more subtle approach might be used. In casual conversation you might wonder aloud about your goals in life while at the same time wondering how you are ever going to afford them. This will have added poignancy if it comes immediately after you have received a positive evaluation or received praise.

- **What motivators will be used to maximize the chance of the message being accepted?**

The seven motivators that drive human decision making are described in chapter 7. That chapter will provide a better understanding of how to tailor messages for maximal influence. For now, two of the seven fundamental motivators will be mentioned for illustrative purposes.

One of the fundamental motivators is consistency. So the fact that a colleague in exactly the same position has already

---

[3] There are clearly some superiors who can be pressured by threats of this nature and some circumstances where an employee is so highly valued he or she can call the tune but generally that is not the case.

received a raise could be usefully inserted into the conversation. This will help, especially if you have been smart enough to previously elicit from the boss comments that compare you favorably to your wealthier colleague. It will also help if, at the precise moment you are making this argument, attention is directed to the sign on the boss's desk which states proudly, "Fairness Above All Else."

Another fundamental motivator is commitment. If you are in the happy position of having received a prior commitment for a raise, now is the time to remind him or her of that. Or, perhaps he or she has not committed to give you a raise per se but has made public a commitment to ensure the best working conditions in the industry.

If at possible, use all seven fundamental motivators to really enhance the power of your presentation. Ways of doing just that are discussed in chapter 7

* **What other communication tools can I use that will maximize the chance of success?**

The use of metaphors, hypnotic language patterns, humor and story-telling could all be invoked to enhance your communication. In wholistic communication it is the total interaction that counts.

The main challenge of purposeful communication is that it needs to be personalized. People vary enormously. What may move one person to action, might alienate another. What might motivate one person, may bore another. In order to be effective communicators we need to be sensitive to our listener's needs. Yet, most of us, have just one predominant communication style. Rather than try to adapt messages, we continue with our communication methods, liking the people who respond to it and believing that we can not get on with those who do not.

Leadership and Purposeful Communication

Good communication is motivation. One of the characteristics of great team leaders and managers is their ability to motivate different personalities. Leaders typically not only recognize individual differences, they adapt their communication accordingly.

Many years ago there was a captain of the English cricket team called Mike Brearley. In cricket, the captain is more than just an honorary title bestowed upon the most charismatic member of the team. A cricket captain makes many important decisions on the field and is constantly handling and motivating the other ten members of his team.

Brearley, a philosopher when he was not playing cricket, was a good cricketer but his skills were no better than many other qualified players. What made Brearley invaluable was his leadership. And what made his leadership so good was his ability to communicate with each player in a way that accounted for that player's personality. Under his captaincy, England achieved good success in large part because of his ability to customize his communication to maximize his team's individualize talents.

Purposeful communication is difficult because, in the final analysis, it involves stepping outside your own boundaries and reaching into another person's world. How well that extension is mastered determines how influential you will be.

Chapter 3

Communication and Spirituality
Learning the power of humility, patience and grace

"And they said, Go to, let us build us a city and tower, whose top may reach into heaven; and let us make us a name, lest we be scattered abroad upon the face of the whole earth

And the Lord came down to see the city and the tower, which the children and men builded.

And the Lord said, Behold, the people is one, and they have all one language; and this they begin to do; and now nothing will be restrained from them, which they have imagined to do.

Go to, let us go down, and there confound their language, that they may not understand one another's speech."

Genesis 11:4-9

According to the bible, the Lord realized that the best way to stop a project dead in its tracks is to prevent the good flow of communication. Moreover, the text acknowledges that if people are united in their communication "nothing will be restrained from them, which they have imagined to do."

Often this story of the Tower of Babel is taken to mean that God gave every man a different language. A one person language is not a language, however, because it has no communication value.

45

We all speak our own language. What confines the ability to communicate is the ego which consists of the habits and entrenched ways of thinking that have become the walls of our mental home. If we stay too confined, living only within those walls, the danger is that we, too, will adopt a one person language and severely limit our communication capacity.

The key to communication, therefore, is the ability to step outside personal confines, to make an effort to truly understand the other person. Such personal extension is the essence of spirituality. Such personal extension is sometimes called love. Sometimes it is called humility. Sometimes it is called a communication skill.

Spirituality is the recognition of a world outside the ego. Spirituality entails the difficult task of suspending judgment and egotistical needs for the sake of understanding another person's thoughts and feelings. Spirituality is the recognition of other cosmic forces greater than personal power. Spiritual beings, therefore, make an attempt to step outside of their own boundaries - such extension is central to spirituality and it is central to good communication.

There are many biblical admonitions to engage in personal extension and ego deferrment. There are for example the edicts to:

Walk a mile in another's shoes

Do Unto Others

Judge not lest ye be judged

If such extension and ego-deferrment were the norm the world would no doubt be a far better place. Stepping outside your box, is not easy, however. Not only do you have to be willing to do it but you also need to understand the forces that shape your thinking and experience. Then, you need to be prepared to face the world without those familiar psychological structures that have supported you since childhood.

Mastery of such extension, however, bestows enormous benefits including a heightened spirituality, a greater chance of happiness and mastery of some essential communication skills.

Stepping Outside The Box

The first task in stepping outside the cage of previous experiences is to understand those personal biases and sensitivities. The keys to understanding these biases are to be aware of characteristic thinking habits and beliefs. It may be strange to consider thought processes are habits but the fact is that we are conditioned to think in the same way that we are conditioned to behave.

Here are some questions that will help identify thinking habits and biases.

Do you keep running into the same problems?

Interpersonal issues are the result of two people, not one. If you keep running into the same problem there is a good chance that you are contributing to those problems. It is often difficult to accept that we might have responsibility for problems especially when it's easy to blame the other person. Repeatedly running into the same problem is a sure sign that you are contributing to it.

For example, a mid level manager with a technology company consulted with me about the difficulty he was having with one of his subordinates. The manager was disappointed because one of his key employees had surprisingly and quickly quit, creating some problems for the management team. My client could not understand why this happened and blamed the alleged irresponsible nature of today's youth for his predicament. After all, the manager told me, he was always positive, upbeat and generous with his praise for all of his subordinates. He was sure that he could not possibly have contributed to the subordinate's departure.

Further analysis showed, however, that he did have some responsibility for the problem. Yes, the manager was always positive, full of praise and upbeat in his evaluations of his charges. That was the problem, he was too upbeat! His euphoria was overdone, creating unrealistic expectations in some of his subordinates. When they realized these expectations were not going to be met, some of his subordinates became frustrated, disenchanted and lost respect for him and the corporation.

Note that the manager's approach would work well for some people but not others. Indeed, their were several subordinates who praised the manager highly and these were, of course, the people that the manager remembered and used to support his view as a competent manager. There had also been others, however, who had been singulalrly unimpressed with his management style.

Although the manager thought he was doing everything right, he was not. In fact, whenever you think you are doing everything right, you are not. There is a wonderful scene in the movie "The Sting." starring Paul Newman and Robert Redford. They have gone to the train station to see the arrival of the target of their con trick, played by Robert Shaw, and his henchmen.

"He's not as big as he thinks he is," says Redford to Newman as they see Shaw arrogantly swagger through the train station with his menacing entourage.

"Neither are we," replies Newman in a wonderful display of humility and insight.

Write down and evaluate your key beliefs
Surprisingly, few people are ever asked to do this simple but important exercise. Many of us are so caught up with the humdrum details of life stuff that we do not stop to consider our real values and priorities.

Having composed the list, consider what implication the choices have for the way you deliver and receive messages. For example, if you have concluded that family is your highest priority, what does that say about how others could effectively communicate with you? Would you be more receptive to messages that addressed you in your family roles? How would you relate to communications by someone who did not share the same values? Are you able to communicate with others who have different values?

Stepping outside your box requires knowing the dimensions of the box and their implications. You have to know your value system and priorities to be a good communicator.

Write a self-description

Generate a list of words that describe you, as you see yourself. Draw up a list of at least twelve adjectives. The more the better.

How do you think other people see you?

How do the significant people in your life see you? What would their description of you look like?

What is your life script?

What stories underpin your identity? Are there specific events that stand out as representative of your identity? For example, when I was a young man playing on the school rugby team, I ran the length of the field to prevent an opponent from scoring and when I caught up with him, I missed the tackle and he scored. For some time this was symbolic for me because it represented a vision of me as someone who put in a lot of hard work but then let opportunity slip through my fingers.

How do you see your life script? Is your story of an underprivileged person made good? Or a privileged person not living up to his or her potential? Or a victim of poor parenting? Or a beneficiary of good parenting?

What positive characteristics have other people generally ascribed to you?

Write down all of the compliments people have made about your skills, personality or character. Which ones do you believe? Do you have hard time believing any compliments?

What negative characteristics have other people generally ascribed to you?

Write down all of the criticisms people have made about your skills, personality or character. Which ones do you believe?

Is there a mismatch between your self-description and other's description of you? Why?

Are you not giving yourself enough credit or are you not facing up to certain realities?

Understanding the confines of your thinking is the most important knowledge you will acquire. These confines represent the filter through which the world is experienced.

Knowing your strengths, weaknesses and biases will help you be as objective as possible when trying to step outside the confines of habitual thinking. This is one reason why therapists are often encouraged to undergo therapy themselves. Therapists have to know their own biases and manage them to be effective counselors. If they can not do this, their counseling will simply be a reflection (and projection) of their own neuroses.

The key here is not expecting to radically change thinking process and personality but to recognize and manage any biases so they do not significantly interfere with your communication skills.

The filters that constrain perception define identity. For example, the perfectionist who rails at you when you make mistakes and is critical of less than perfect performance *beats themselves up even more harshly for the same imperfect behavior.*

External dialog is a reflection of internal dialog

The inability to step outside the box leads to projection – the biggest enemy of communication and the destroyer of relationships.

Projection

Human beings have an automatic tendency to interpret events. Such interpretation is essential for survival, which depends on making the most adaptive response to the environment as quickly as possible.

These interpretations bear the imprint of our biases and the fact that this process is automatic means that other view points are rarely considered. We thus jump to conclusions about the behavior and motivation of others based as much on our own biases as their behavior.

Miscommunication and alienation are the most common results of basing interpretations on our own biases rather than an objective appraisal of others behavior. In a famous social psychology study, arrangements were made for a gunman to burst into the lecture hall in the middle of his lecture, fire two shots and then leave. Observers were then asked to report exactly what they saw. The results showed enormous variability in the reports of those who witnessed the event. The number of shots, the number of gunmen, the amount of time they were there, their departure and their motives were all open to interpretation and generated many different responses.

Perception is influenced by a whole host of factors. For example, perception can be dramatically altered by the sequence in which events are observed or revealed. For example,

"He stole the medicine. He got caught. He felt guilty."

"He stole the medicine. He felt guilty. He got caught."

Perception can also be dramatically altered by providing one extra piece of information. For example,

"He stole the medicine. He got caught. He felt guilty even though he knew that stealing the medicine was the only way he could save his mother."

51

Not only do we project, we hardly ever do a reality check. If we did conduct a reality check we would discover that much of the time our interpretations are downright wrong.

Judge not lest ye be wrong

Even when you are right, stopping to test the reality of interpretations (for example, by asking the other person what is really on their mind) has tremendous symbolic value. Reality checking implies a desire for understanding.

One of the great values of listening is that it provides a reality check on interpretations. Of course, sometimes even the reality check is itself subject to bias.

How to objectively check your interpretations
Repeat back listener's words to them
Find out listener's interpretation
Seek evidence for your interpretation
Is your interpretation always similar, in other words a habit?

Humility, Patience and Grace

Stepping outside of your cage requires courage. It requires the suspension of ego protective devices and old habits. Here are twenty actions you can take that will help you begin to step out of the cage of your own ego.

1. Let others in front of you.

Allow pushy drivers in, give up your seat and allow others with less shopping to go to the check out in front of you.

2. **Remember your manners.**
    Say please and thank you, take your hat off when you enter a building and hold doors open for others

3. **Tell everyone to keep the change.**
    During the course of the day let everyone who owes you small change, keep it.

4. **Respect your Elders.**
    Call your grandparents and look for ways to help elderly people you encounter.

5. **Only drink water.**
    Unless otherwise medically indicated, spend one day just drinking water and eating nothing. If that's too difficult, eat but only drink water.

6. **Slow down and plant the roses**
    Take time to plant a flower. If you cannot plant, ensure that you give someone a flower. Schedule downtime during the day.

7. **Find the positive.**
    Seek the most positive interpretation of events, find beauty and assume the best.

8. **Seek the farthest space in the parking lot.**
    Defer to others and benefit from the walk.

9. **If you think your lot is bad, visit the less fortunate.**
    Go to the cancer ward, retirement home infirmary, children's hospital and /or speak to the homeless

10. Say hello or at least smile to everyone.
Keep your head up and offer warm greetings to everyone you see.

11. Say your prayers.
Talk to your god and ask for his help and forgiveness.

12. Spend at least fifteen minutes looking at the stars.
Look up, look out and look beyond.

13. Listen to the birds
Are they talking to each other and if so, how do they do that?

14. Practice deep breathing/meditate.
Take time through the day to close your eyes, slow your breathing and listen to your thoughts

15. Examine your body.
Feel your skin, touch your tongue and listen to your heart.

16. Look at photos of your children when they were babies.
Reconnect with the power and awe of the passage of time. If you do not have photos or children, think about your childhood and development.

17. Read the Bible.
  Turn to any page and read from your holy book. What does the passage say and what does it mean to you?

18. Speak to your priest.
  Have a conversation with your spiritual advisor. If you do not have a spiritual advisor, seek and ye shall find.

19. Tell people close to you that you love them.
  Use the words, "I love you," and don't blush.

20. Look in the mirror.
  Like what you see but recognize there is always room for improvement.

  Now, you are ready to tackle the difficult but rewarding task of listening.

Chapter 4

Listening
The best defense is the worst offense

Why do so few people listen properly? Apart from the fact that few people are ever taught good listening skills and egocentric, expressive communication predominates, there are several other reasons why good listening is resisted.

First, some are so narcissistic that they find it difficult to empathize. The idea of another viewpoint is so threatening that it simply cannot be embraced. Not only is such narcissism defensiveness in the extreme, it is the death of communication and highly offensive.

Second, others are able to empathize and appreciate other viewpoints but resist doing so because it is too threatening. After all, listening might lead to understanding and from there it is but a short step to accepting another viewpoint.

Listening is not capitulating. On the contrary, it will help your communication and improve the chances of being influential.

Listening is not accepting. Understanding and tolerance are two completely different concepts that often get confused. Just because the forces shaping behavior can be understood does not mean that it makes that behavior tolerable or acceptable.

"Understanding is a two-way street" -- Eleanor Roosevelt.

The key skill for the good communicator is listening. Purposeful communication requires customized messages that can only be generated with knowledge of the audience.

You can never have enough knowledge of an audience any more than you can ever have enough knowledge of a fiance(e). Knowledge of the audience's position on the topic under discussion and of them as a person are both essential.

Understanding the listener's language and incorporating it into communications makes it far more likely that your message will be understood and accepted. The listener's language is not just the words they use, but the meaning of the words and the emotional associations that exist with those words. Words and thus ideas, are tied in to experience. The effective communicator links his message to the listener's experience, ideally their key experiences.

If people are allowed to talk, they will reveal an incredible amount about themselves. People like to talk about themselves because they seldom get an opportunity to do so. There's the well-worn anecdote of the traveler who engages his fellow airplane passenger in a conversation. The passenger talk non-stop for two hours and when they depart company turns to the traveler and says, "You're a great conversationalist!"

Listening consists of two key elements.-- what to listen for and how to do it.

What to listen for?
The audience has the keys to effective communication. By listening to them, important clues will be gained about how to customize your message. When listening, attention needs to be focused on the following.

Content
What are they saying?
What is their position on the topic under discussion?
What arguments are they using?

What are their goals?
What emotions are being expressed and where do they occur and where are they emphasized. Are they showing anger, fear, delight? What is behind these feelings?

Background
What are their interests?
What is important to them. After listening, do you have an idea of the person's priorities, goals and values?
Who is important to them? What sort of people do they like? What sort of people do they dislike?
What do they like about themselves?
What do they feel their shortcomings are?
Has their been reference to any personal experiences or specific events?
Has there been reference to personal details?

Their interests will also give you a clue as to they preferred senses. Do they like music, physical activity, cooking, sculpting, painting, - all of which use a predominant sense.

Background variables are important, especially some of the more obvious ones. Personal variables that influence ideas and behavior include gender, age, socio-economic status, marital status, cultural background, religion, parent status, education and occupation.

Form
What ideas elicit what emotions?
What metaphors, analogies etc., are used.
What makes them laugh?
Have any special words or phrases been used that seem important?
Do they express humor? If so, how?
What senses do they refer to? E.g Do they talk about touching, hearing, seeing, smelling, tasting?

For example, if someone is talking about how close they were to reaching a goal do they say..

I was so close I could almost touch it.
I was so close I could almost feel it.
I was so close I could almost taste it.
I was so close I could almost smell it.
I was so close I could almost see it.

Observation

Listening also entails observing. Non verbal communication tells you much about a person. Specific behaviors to look for include the following.

Foot-flapping. This is typically an anxiety or discomfort reaction, implying the foot flapper wants to leave the situation.

Nose touching. This can sometimes mean that the person is not being completely honest or has some anxiety about being exposed. The erectile tissue in the nose is said to swell during lying, creating this nose-touching behavior and the story of Pinnochio.

Leaning away. This body movement often implies a desire to distance him or herself from you. Leaning towards you has the opposite connotation.

Crouched or hunched posture implies defensiveness.

Facial expression. What is the speaker talking about when they smile, frown? Pay special attention to what is being said the moment that emotion is detected. If a client shows strong emotion, I often ask what they were thinking at that precise moment.

You can get a lot of information if you are in the listener's environment -- home, car, office. For example, here are some pointers to look for if you are in someone's office

Do they have photos on a desk? Who is in the photos?

Is their environment neat and tidy or cluttered.?

Where is their desk situated? Is the desk facing the door to invite guests in or away from it to discourage them?

What other chairs are there? How are they arranged? Are they big or small?

What is on the wall? Artwork? Is any music playing? Are there any books? If so, what?

Are there any inspirational sayings, jokes, motivational prompts etc on the walls or on the desk?

What awards, degrees, professional qualifications or licenses?

Questions to ask (subtly, of course)

With all of the above in mind, here are fifty questions that will reveal much about a person. It is unlikely you will get a chance to actually ask all fifty even though that does make for an interesting conversation. The questions do give an idea of what to look for, however. The questions do not have to be asked as they are presented below but rather should flow as part of normal conversation. To start, answer the questions as they apply to you.

Fifty Fun Fact Finders

1. What is your greatest personal achievement?
2. What is your greatest professional achievement?
3. What was the funniest moment?
4. What was the saddest moment?
5. What was school like?
6. What was/is your role in your family?
7. Who is your favorite historical figure?
8. What is your favorite movie?
9. What is your favorite book?
10. What are your strengths?
11. What hobbies do you have?
12. What is your favorite food?

13. What is your favorite drink?
14. What senses are your strongest?
15. If you were an animal what would you be?
16. Do you have/own your own pet?
17. What are your favorite places?
18. What was your scariest moment?
19. What is your ideal job/profession/career?
20. Do you believe in God?
21. Do you regularly attend church of any kind?
22. Do you say prayers?
23. What is your favorite physical activity?
24. If you could re-live an age, what age would that be?
25. If you could move forward or back in time, which would it be? What era?
26. What is your favorite color?
27. What is your favorite car?
28. What is your favorite smell?
29. What is your favorite music? Type and piece?
30. Do you have a recurrent dream? What is it?
31. What is your favorite fairy tale?
32. Which TV channel do you watch the most?
33. What is your favorite time of day?
34. What is your favorite meal?
35. If you were a historical figure who would you be?
36. If you were a cultural figure (movie star, singer, personality, sports star etc..) who would you be?
37. How do you want to be remembered? Obituary?
38. What is your favorite taste?
39. If you could speak another language what would it be?
40. What part of the newspaper do you read first?
41. What's more important to you, recognition or money?
42. If you knew you only had one year left to live, how would you spend it?
43. What is your favorite word?
44. What is your least favorite word?
45. What is your favorite swear word?
46. What's your earliest memory?

47. What was your scariest moment?
48. What's your biggest regret?
49. What are your goals for the next year?
50. If you could spend one day with anyone who would that be?

How to Listen

When listening you need to be actively leading the conversation so that the other person will reveal as much as possible about themselves. Of course, if you are simply encouraging them to talk successfully, they will be disclosing much that will help you understand them. This isn't just a manipulative ploy to give you a communication advantage. You are simply getting to know another person.

When listening do the following

Avoid making judgments about what you are hearing. Use your mind to fully concentrate on what is being said and the interconnections between the ideas so that a full picture of the person can be created

Stay focused. Do not let your attention wander and certainly do not do anything else. There's nothing more off putting than having a conversation with someone while they are watching TV or reading the paper. You can not do two things at once.

Look interested. Use eye-contact, stay relaxed and lean slightly towards the person talking.

Do not interrupt. Do ask for clarification if you are uncertain about a particular point.

Smile. You do not need to be a laughing hyena but a smile always makes other feel good and reinforces behavior, in this case, self revelation.

Give compliments. There's no need to overdo this but when appropriate, provide positive empathic responses. For example, if someone has just described a feat of which they are proud, you might say something like..

"I can see why you are proud of that achievement.." or

'That must have taken some doing.." or

"I bet there are only a few people who can say that."

Find points of similarity. Look for the ways in which you and the other person share similar experiences.

Share. If you can identify with the talker, take the opportunity to share your version of similar events.

Reflect in a positive manner. Try the technique of simply restating back to the person what he or she has just said to you. If you do this in a positive manner you'll be amazed at the reaction you get!

Remember at least the main points and the parts that seemed most important to the speaker. You should be able to restate the main arguments and points back to the speaker when he or she has finished.

As you can see, listening requires tremendous effort. When I have been listening to a client for an hour I am really tired from the effort of concentration needed to listen to every word, watch for non verbal cues and emotions, and memorize significant details.

Once you have understood more about your audience you are in a better position to employ specific tools to communicate more effectively.

Chapter 5

Generating an Emotional Response
Experiencing is believing

The thesis of this book is that the experience is the message. Behavior is driven by emotions, so successful communication entails generating an emotional response that will enable the listener to relate to, and then act on, your message.

This principle is used all the time in everyday life, even if those using it do not articulate the principle in quite the same way a stated above. For example...

A suitor is made jealous to appreciate what he might be losing

An athlete is criticized in order to fire up his competitive instincts.

Good communicators are motivators constantly looking for ways to incite their audiences and listeners into action. So what tools can be used to purposefully generate emotional responses that lead to actions?

The tools of influence are as follows.

- Story-telling
- Associations
- Identification
- Likability
- Humor
- Metaphors

- Words

Story-telling

Any communication can be made into a story. For example, several years ago I discovered that onions disagreed with me. So, whenever I go into a restaurant I have to inquire about the onion content and then convince the server to provide my order onion free. This is no easy task because many servers are either so overworked or so much creatures of habit that my request has left their head before they have even got back to the kitchen.

I discovered that if I say to the server: "Please can you hold the onions," I get an onion free meal about 65% of the time. So I have got used to saying the following which never fails to get the desired, onion-free result.

I am allergic to onions and I will die if I eat any of them. You will be then faced with the embarrassing and difficult task of removing my body as secretively as possible lest any of your other customers draws the wrong conclusions about the healthiness of your food.

Of course, I say this with my tongue planted firmly in my cheek but the image of having to remove a dead body from the restaurant is clearly effective in getting the server to remember and check about the onion status of my meal.

Stories and Themes

Every story has a theme. In the movies, this theme is almost always reflected in a line of script at an important part of the action and often repeated throughout.

In Angels in the Outfield, several times in the movie the line "You never know, it could happen," is repeated and indeed the movie is about faith and belief.

In The Lion King, when Simba faces his own reflection and is undergoing extreme self-doubt, his father appears to him and reminds him to "remember who you are." The movie is about identity and heritage.

The need for human beings to interpret their environment has already been described. The listener will make their own interpretations of your communication. The effective communicator guides the listener to the desired interpretation.

The innate need for making sense of the environment and finding meaning in it is the reason why stories and story-telling are so fascinating. One of the reason why movies are so popular is that they provide interpretations of life that are very acceptable to us because they almost always have a happy ending. Nobody wants to pay $6 for a movie to find out that that life is tough.

Great story-tellers control the audience's interpretation by using specific devices. They leave little ambiguity about the meaning of the story.

• Stories are good communications in that they elicit emotions.

• Stories use symbolism and metaphor that overcome any resistance to the underlying message.

• ~~Good~~ Stories generally have a satisfactory outcome. The ending is critical because it determines the overall meaning of the story.

• A story consists of three parts: A protagonist (a hero or central figure) with a goal, an obstacle to the achievement of that goal (conflict), and a (typically successful) resolution of that conflict.

• Stories use the natural interpretative powers of human beings to lead the listener/viewer through particular feelings to a certain emotional state.

Any minor event can be turned into a story. Turning everyday events into stories is a useful exercise. For example, consider these different versions of the same event.

Version #1.

I sent my seven year-old to the store to buy some bagels and he came back with a loaf of bread.

Version#2.

I sent my seven year-old to the store to buy bagels. He could not find any, so not wanting to return empty-handed, he bought some bread instead.

Version#3.

I sent my seven year-old to the store to buy bagels. It was the first time he had been to the store on his own and he was anxious to show that he could be trusted with such an adult task. When he got to the store he went directly to where he knew the bagels were displayed. Oh No! To his horror he found that there were no bagels left! He looked frantically all over the store to find some, but the more he looked, the more upset he became. After a long fruitless search and almost in despair he decided to buy some bread instead. On the way home he was almost in tears, worrying whether he had done the right thing. After all, he had gone to get bagels and was coming home with bread. Anxiously he entered the kitchen where I was waiting. He stood there in silence for a while, hiding the bread behind his back. Eventually, barely holding back the tears, he announced that there were no bagels. I told him that he had done a great job. "Son, " I said, "You can't always get what you want. You have to adapt. You made an excellent choice. I am proud of you!"

In the everyday, we do not spend time focusing on the underlying symbolic meaning of events. Clearly, we can not seek deep symbolism in everything we do every minute of the day, but we do far too little of it and thus become disconnected from the true meaning in our lives. When we become disconnected from the true meaning in our lives, we lose our motivation to do important things.

Stories elicit emotions. The first version of the story is factual and makes no attempt to elicit emotion. Readers of the story might have some emotional response but *they* will provide it rather than the story-teller. The story does not guide readers to a specific emotional place and, as a result, there could be as many emotional responses and interpretations as there are readers. Some readers might feel angered by the apparent carelessness of the child, others might be amused and yet others might feel frustrated.

In the second version, more information is provided that will lead the listener in a particular direction but a lot of the interpretation and meaning is still left to the listener's discretion.

In the third version, the reader is guided to feel certain emotions. The reader with empathy might feel the anxiety of the child trying to please, the frustration that comes when the simplest of expectations is not met, doubt in an unfamiliar situation, relief when uncertainty is resolved.

The religious building site

I was recently passing a building site that belonged to the church. It was near the end of the day and there were three workers still laboring on the site. I asked the first man what he was doing.

"I'm laying some bricks out for this wall," he replied

I asked the second man what he was doing.

"I'm fixing the cement," he replied.

A third man was carrying bricks across the lot in a wheelbarrow. I asked him what he was doing.

"I'm building a cathedral," he replied.

Although individuals vary to the degree to which they are sensitive to these various emotions, almost everyone has experienced the whole gamut of emotions by the time they are out of childhood. In other words, almost all of us can be hooked. Despite large gender differences in the feeling of empathy -- women have far more empathic capacity than men -- men are still capable of empathy even if it is not experienced in the same way as women.

For a large part of my career I have worked in the field of addictions.[4] I have never had an alcohol or drug problem which has prompted the criticism that I am thus not qualified to treat it. The criticism misses the point. Although I have not had a drug or alcohol problem I have experienced shame, guilt, deceit, compulsion, conflict, anger and the whole range of other emotions that accompany addiction problems. Not having an alcohol problem does not disqualify me as a healer of these problems. Not feeling the emotions, and thus being able to empathize, would.

Creating the right emotional response is therefore critical in effective communication. When providing communication en masse, the story will try to elicit emotions using situations for a general audience. In one-on-one communication, you can target emotions using specific situations that through effective listening, are known to be specially important to the listener.

For example, suppose your listener is very sensitive to the notion of fairness. Through diligent listening you know that her childhood was characterized by very unfair treatment. As a result, she is sensitive to fairness and the emotions created by its presence or absence.

You can invest a message to this listener with enormous energy and power if you appeal to her sense of fairness even when delivering bad news.

---

[4] Just for the record, my Ph.D in clincial psychology awarded by the University of London, which took six years of my life, is entitled The Behavioral Assessment and Treatment of Alcohol Dependence.

For example..

"I know there were extenuating circumstances but unfortunately you have to re-take the class."

"I know that there were extenuating circumstances but it would simply be unfair to anyone who has taken this course, or who is yet to take it, to allow you to pass without completing the course work."

Although mediated biochemically, there is strong evidence that all emotions are a result of social perceptions. People vary in their interpretations of social events, so two people can view the same event and feel completely different, even completely opposite, emotions.

Here is a list of emotions and the social perceptions that engender them.

Perception	Emotion
Unfairness	Anger
Thwarted effort	Frustration
Threat, immediate or future	Anxiety
Loss	Sadness
Violation of moral standard	Guilt, shame
Anticipation of positive	Excitement

Situations that generate these perceptions can be created to elicit emotions that are going to be the most efficient vehicles of your message.

Associations

Despite its enormous complexity, the human nervous system works on two remarkably simple principles – association and repetition. While the works of Pavlov may not make you salivate, they were illuminating in showing the tremendous power of association. Simply put, when two events happen together enough of the time, one event will have the power to elicit the other. Sensations are encoded sequentially which means that significant events are paired with the circumstances that surround them and one has the power to elicit the other. This is especially true for traumatic or very meaningful events.

Many years ago while visiting Italy, I took a boat back from the Isle of Capri to the mainland. I was eating cherry yogurt on the deck of this boat while simultaneously acrid smoke from a diesel engine was belching out from the funnel. For many years, the thought of cherry yogurt reflexively elicited in me nauseating sensations of diesel smoke. It is only recently that I have been able to disassociate these two sensations.

The power of an event to elicit a specific emotion is dependent on a number of factors.

Novelty. If I had been a regular eater of cherry yogurt and it was thus associated with a whole variety of other sensations, the association with diesel smoke would not have been so profound.

Level of arousal. The more traumatic an event is, the more simultaneous events are likely to be associated with it. This clearly has survival value. Learning the warning signs of a dangerous situation is adaptive. As a result, traumatic experiences are very rich in their associative potential. Those who have been exposed to trauma have vivid recollections of the environment at the time of the trauma across the whole spectrum of their senses. It is adaptive to heighten senses at times of trauma simply to learn the warning signs associated with the traumatic experience.

Preparedness. Certain associations are hot wired in the nervous system because they confer survival advantages. Studies on aversion have shown that food is more highly prepared for associations with feelings of nausea than electric shock. When electric shock is paired with a certain food, animals show little aversion to the food. When nausea is paired with the same food , animals show almost complete aversion to the food in question.

On the boat from Capri, the diesel fumes were making me nauseated thus turning me off cherry yogurt for two decades.[5]

So how the power of association be used to enhance communications?

First, associations can be made that will remind the listener of important messages. Using everyday stimuli as motivational prompts and reminders by pairing them with important messages is a valuable tactic. For example, recently, I consulted with a local fitness club. After observing a spinning class[6] and its tremendously powerful impact, I suggested the following.

At the end of the class, the participants were almost euphoric, having had both a great physical work-out and a tremendous social experience. How great if that feeling could be captured in some way -- almost as if it were being bottled.

I set about creating an association with that feeling. The two objects that were naturally used at the end of the session when the participants were feeling good, were water bottles and towels. I trained the instructors to end the session with a very ritualized association. When everyone was feeling great, the instructors were trained to get the participants to towel themselves down. The instructors were trained to get everyone to do this at the same time with the following commentary.

"Take your white towel. Feel the softness of that towel and concentrate on how wonderful you feel as the towel absorbs the signs of your wonderful work-out. As the towel caresses you , feel great about how you have taken care of yourself today."

---

[5] Such taste aversions are quite common and are testament to the power of experience over logic. Even though I knew that my nausea was a result of diesel fumes it did not change my reaction when eating the yogurt a long way from Capri, in a diesel free environment.
[6] Spinning is an a activity where groups are led through synchronous exercises on indoor bicycles

The same effect could be reached using music, although the music would have to be suitably unfamiliar and thus not associated with other feelings to derive any significant effect. It is also possible to create associations using other senses. Perhaps a certain sort of air freshener could be sprayed in order to create an association between a certain fragrance and the experience. In any event, strong sensory impressions relating to the towel were created and associated with the feeling of well-being. With enough repetition, the towel itself would help elicit the feeling of well-being and thus act as a reminder of the value and meaning of the work-out. The towel is now associated with the euphoria of the work-out and can be used as a motivational prompt away from the health club. This is especially useful on days when the participant may be resistant to working out. After a few repetitions of this association procedure several participants claimed that it did come to have that motivating effect.

Such associations are unwittingly created all the time. A child uses his pillow as a punch bag to vent his anger and then wonder why he has difficulty sleeping on it. He or she is literally sleeping on their anger.

How does this work in a business setting? The business lunch and the executive golf game are both examples of association in action. The business lunch was not just designed to elicit the client's obligation by use of the principle of reciprocity. The business lunch is designed to make clients associate the positive feelings that accompany a good meal with the message that the host is trying to convey. It is an attempt to correlate your presence and message with a positive emotional state. Eating good food is pleasurable.

There are many other ways in which businesses attempt to create associations in the consumer's mind. The stronger the association the more automatic the connection. For example, with repeated exposure who does not see the Nike swoosh and think of that company and its slogan? It's so automatic, we just do it. Music, distinctive slogans, packaging and even celebrity spokespersons all, with enough repetition, create associations which do two things. One, they make the consumer feel positive about the product.

74

They also make the consumer familiar with the product. We are much more likely to accept and thus buy products that are familiar to us.

Familiarity breeds consent

The power of association also tells you something about how to pair, or not pair messages. Any part of a paired message is going to be influenced by the other message with which it is paired. It does not matter whether the two messages are *logically* linked. If you deliver them together they will be *experientially* linked.

For example, if you were to simultaneously inform an employee of a pay raise and an undesirable change in working conditions, the two would be inevitably linked in the employee's mind even if they were logically totally separate.

Individually, each of us have our unique associations with a whole host of environmental stimuli. Places, smells, sights and words will all have specific associations. In the case of words, the communicator needs to be sure that words that have the right associations are used.

Language

Words have emotional connotations. The right words can effectively elicit emotion and create the right experience.

The fitness class mentioned above was the setting for a good example of the emotions carried by concepts. In the spinning class just mentioned, the fitness professionals used visualization techniques. One of the instructors had devised her own visualization that consisted of imagining a bike tour in the area surrounding the health club where the spinning class was taking place. The instructor guided them through various landmarks including the nearby hospital which she described in some detail.

At the end of the session many of the participants expressed dislike at the guided imagery. One spinner was actually in tears at the back of the room. Why?

Unfortunately, the group leader failed to appreciate the associative power of the image of the hospital. Taking people on an imaginal bike tour of the hospital also opens them up to all their associations with the word 'hospital', the concept 'hospital' and their experiences at this particular hospital. Hospitals generally are not happy places so it is no surprise that many will have unpleasant feelings and thoughts when they think of hospitals.

Such associations might be unconscious or they might be very conscious. The fact is, however, that words contain tremendous power to elicit emotions. There is a whole art form dedicated to the associative power of words - it is called poetry.

In my seminars on communication I make the following presentation.

First I ask the attendees to read the following list of words.

Happy	Party	Celebration
Humor	Joke	Fun
Enjoyment	Smile	Vacation
Laughter	Hope	Ecstasy

Then I ask the attendees to read the following list

Sad	Loss	Disease
Trauma	Misery	Tears
Upset	Distress	Illness
Anger	Frustration	Trouble

The difference in facial expressions as these two lists are read are quite amazing. When attendees read the first list, they are smiling and the postures are open. When they read the second list, their postures are slumped and frowns appear.

Words automatically convey emotional content. The sounds of words create associations which have meaning. For example, in the business letter from the HMO mentioned earlier, the use of the word "staff" was changed because it sounds like "staph" which is an infection. Be aware of the sounds, associations and emotional connotations of words.

Metaphors

A metaphor is a word or phrase representing an object or idea in place of another by way of suggesting a likeness between them.

Consider the following examples.

A tidal wave of enthusiasm
A waterfall of enthusiasm
A trickle of enthusiasm

Each of the metaphors connotes visual images and has emotional associations that lead the reader to a different experiential space. A tidal wave engulfs everything in its path and is frightening in its size and power. A waterfall is a continuous cascade that seemingly never stops. You can almost hear the water cascading. A trickle could dry up at any moment. Metaphors paint mental pictures and carry emotional power.

Metaphors work in ways other than merely painting pictures. Some of the time our conscious mind does not allow us to express inner thoughts and feelings. This is often because we do not want to acknowledge them ourselves or to anyone else. Sometimes we are not even sure what those inner thoughts and feelings are. Our conscious filter will not allow us to shine the light on the inner workings of the mind. We have to go beyond the conscious barrier.

Talking metaphorically allows us to express these thoughts and feelings in the safety of not articulating them directly.

One time I was trying to convey a psychological concept to one of my students. For some reason she was not able to grasp what

I was saying. After a few minutes struggling with the concept, the student looked out of the window and said, "It's foggy out there." Obviously it was foggy in there (her head), too.

A couple presented to me with marital problems but are defensive in talking about their sex life. No matter how hard I tried, they stubbornly resist talking about intimacy. Recognizing the relationship between eating and sex, I then ask the wife to tell me about the differences between her and her husband at the dinner table.

"Oh, we're quite different," said the wife. "He dives in and is finished before I even have a chance to get started!"

In the same way, metaphorical messages also allow us to receive messages that our conscious mind would reject. Metaphors allow the presentation of messages that go beyond the conscious barrier and thus by-pass resistance.

The use of metaphors is so powerful that there is a whole discipline dedicated to the design of therapeutic metaphors and metaphorical stories.

I experienced the following metaphorical story when I attended a workshop run by David Lee, one of the leaders in this field.[7] The essence of the story is Lee's and I have paraphrased it here. This story would be helpful for someone struggling with changing an abusive situation or suffering from lack of assertiveness.

In a clinical situation, the client listens to these stories in a state of deep relaxation. Reading it, however, will give some sense of how these stories are constructed and their effect.

" A woman is called to the office early by her boss. She is conscientious and hates to be late so she ensures that she arrives a

---

[7] Lee is the co-founder of the Northeast NLP Institute in Kennebunk, Maine.

good hour before her normal work start. When she gets there her boss isn't even there yet so she waits patiently for him to arrive. Eventually, when he does arrive, he barely acknowledges her. While she is still waiting she hears her boss make a phone call to a friend and start an animated conversation about last weekend's golf game.

By now she has been waiting for him for thirty minutes. The phone conversation about golf continues. Another ten minutes elapse. During this time the woman cannot help thinking about how abusive her boss is to her. He has never given her a raise despite the importance of her work and her competence. He never acknowledges her work and last year promoted a lesser employee over her.

Another ten minutes elapse and the golf conversation continues. Her friends have told her she should quit, that she could easily find another job. She is however, loyal to a fault and finds the idea of change hard. She has never been one for confrontation. She follows the rules without complaint.

The golf conversation continues. She has been waiting an hour! There was no need for her to come in early at all. Perhaps he asked her to be in early just to make her do it!

Frustrated, she retrieves the morning paper. As she turns the pages, a story attracts her attention. The story is about a circus. The woman has fond memories of the circus. When she was a child she went every year with her father who told everything there was to know about the circus animals. He explained how the lions were trained and how the elephants are tied up using the thinnest ropes. When they are young they are tied with the thin ropes and beaten if they tried to escape. Eventually the thin ropes keep them in place even though the elephants are easily strong enough to break free. But they don't.

As the golf conversation continues inside the boss's office, the woman reads the story. There had been a fire in the circus. The fire spread and threatened the animals. The horses quickly bolted,

79

the chimpanzees ran off. It was only when the fire was almost upon them that the elephants finally broke free – surprisingly easily from the thin ropes that contained them.

The woman put down the paper. She scribbled a short note to her boss that simply said "I quit," and left."

The beautiful thing about metaphors and metaphorical stories is that they do not need or benefit from running commentary or explanation. Suffice to say, therefore, that the metaphorical elements of the story reflected the feelings that feed helplessness and provide behavioral strategies necessary to break the problem at hand, which in this case, was lack of assertiveness.

The message of the story could consciously be conveyed thus.

"You have simply been trained to stay in an abusive situation. You have the power to leave it. Just do it and you'll see how easy it is."

That message is almost certain to be less influential than the metaphor because:

1. It is someone else's opinion. The message has not been arrived at by the women herself

2. It is too conscious allowing resistance to block acceptance.

Devising Metaphors and Stories

The likeness between the metaphor and the concept to which it is linked contains the sensory information that elicits the emotional response. To construct a metaphor, you need to decide what emotional response is to be elicited and then consider the objects that convey those feelings. The metaphorical representation of abstract ideas is powerful because we live in a physical world.

80

Physical objects thus have a sensory reality to us which is essential for our experience.[8]

Create a metaphor by completing the sentence

Good service is like....

Management is like....

Our company is like....

Parenting is like...

(Suggestions provided in the appendix)

While the creation of stories and metaphors may seem like a daunting task, there are several steps that will guide their creation. Like all creative efforts, there are fundamental techniques that help direct creativity.

First, there are some questions that need to be answered.

What mental state or attitude exists now that is targeted for change?

What new mental state or attitude needs to be attained?

What resources are needed to make the change?

What experiences are needed to effect this change?

Suppose you are trying to motivate someone who is having serious doubts and little success, to persist with a course of action. This is a universal situation and could apply to a colleague, a student, a friend, a teammate, --anyone.

---

[8] It is precisely because we derive reality from the physical world that the French philosopher Dreyfus wrote a paper entitled "Why computers need bodies in order to be intelligent."

The answers to the questions above are...

Current mental state...defeated

Targeted mental state...hope

Resources needed...persistence, faith

Experiences needed...success, sense of control

The next question is:

What life experiences are similar to the ones needed to effect the psychological changes in question?

For example, what other stories reflect the use of persistence, faith and planning to build confidence?

There are many examples to chose from. A story could simply be constructed about a person who overcame overwhelming odds to be a success. Real life examples abound in every area of life from Franklin D Roosevelt to Wilmer Rudolph. The example needs to mirror as much as possible the shifts required of the person in question. So a story about someone moving from defeat to hope and success using persistence, planning and faith would be the most beneficial.

The story could be about you, the communicator. For example, I might relay the following to someone in this situation.

"When I was studying for my Ph.D I reached a low point when I thought I would never get it finished. I was completely bogged down and saw no way I could get it done. My thesis seemed like a mammoth wall that surrounded me and blocked everything in front of me.

"I just decide to keep plodding away, chipping away a bit here and a bit there even though I had no confidence that it would ever make a difference. I just decided to take one step at a time and not even look up at that wall.

"One day I did look up at that wall and found that many of the bricks had now been removed. For the first time, I felt as if I could dismantle this huge obstruction. I could see clearly, that following a specific plan of action I could dismantle the whole wall! I can't tell you what great feeling that was!"

If the story or metaphor can come from the person's own experience, so much the better. For example, you might remind the person thus.

"You remember when you were trying to learn the piano (or ride a bike, drive a car, master any sort of skill or learn a subject). Remember how in the beginning you felt you were never going to be able to do it. But you stuck with it, practiced long and hard and eventually found success."

You can also use cultural metaphors, stories and movies to make the same point. A wonderful movie and real life event that captures the resources needed to snatch victory from the jaws of defeat is Apollo 13. The entire movie is a metaphor for coping and the use of persistence, planning, faith and taking one step at a time to foster hope and ultimately success.

As the resources and transitions are considered, various obvious metaphors come into mind.

Taking one step at a time conjures up images of ladders, or mountaineers painstakingly working their way up a mountain, step by treacherous step.

Having faith is like climbing that mountain or ladder and not looking down but staying focused on the next step.

Having a plan conjures up images of blueprints, architectural drawings, technical designs and battle strategies.

As you begin to brainstorm these ideas, the metaphors and stories begin to suggest themselves. Fine tuning them to make them personally meaningful is the difference between a good metaphor and a really effective one.

Metaphorical Action

Actions speak louder than words. Consider this syndicated story reported thus:

"Press Secretary eats 'toxic' fish

Greenpeace activists tried to make a point by delivering Gov. Mike Foster a free lunch of fish from a polluted bayou Thursday. Foster's press secretary did them one better: She ate it.

About 40 activists rallied to bring attention to what they said was terrible pollution in Louisiana, particularly near several petrochemical plants along the Mississippi River between Baton Rouge and New Orleans.

With television cameras rolling, the activists went to the Governor's mansion with what they called a toxic lunch: fish from a bayou near a plastics plant where signs warn against eating the catch. The governor wasn't home, but his press secretary, Marsanne Golsby, whipped a plastic fork out of her pocket and ate the fish. Several of the activist warned her to stop, telling her where the fish came from.

"Why did you bring it if you didn't want me to eat it? Golsby asked.

When contacted later, Golsby said she felt just fine."

Press secretary Golsby pulled a masterful stroke of communication. No-one knows whether she ever did get sick and maybe in fifteen years she'll click a lot and glow in the dark. But for right now, she completely trumped the public relations move of the environmental protesters.

Consider this example.

A friend of man was an outstanding salesperson for a major corporation. Once, while in an important business meeting waiting to deliver a significant presentation, an employee from the hotel interrupted the meeting. The employee announced that a car in the parking lot had rolled from its space, crashed into the retaining wall and had suffered significant damage. "Did the car belong to anyone in the room?" The employee asked.

Without missing a beat my friend stood up.

"It's mine," he announced. "Will it be okay if I attend to it in about an hour or so? The presentation I'm about to give is far more important than my car."

How do you evaluate his reaction? If it is his car, he has shown remarkable commitment to his work priorities and tremendous focus on the task at hand. If it isn't his car, he has shown admirable opportunism and quick thinking!

Belief

A critical part of communication is the conviction with which the message is conveyed. Belief can be communicated in many ways.

Enthusiasm. A message delivered without enthusiasm is a half-hearted communication likely to convince no-one. However, there is enthusiasm and there is mock enthusiasm. Mock enthusiasm is often displayed by tele-marketers whose whole presentation borders on the manic, partly because tele-marketers are trying to make as many calls as possible in the shortest amount of time. Most of us have come to understand that such mock enthusiasm precedes a sales pitch and our defenses go up immediately. It would be better for the tele-marketer to be as sincere and friendly as possible when introducing themselves and step up the enthusiasm when talking about the product or service they are trying to sell.[9]

---

[9] Is enthusiasm trained in your organization. If so, how and to whom?

Action. The most convincing message that you believe in a product or service is that you actually use it yourself. If you do not do what you are asking potential clients to do, there's no chance of gaining compliance.

In drives for charitable funds, the solicitor for the funds has be a significant contributor (unless they are paid professionals in which case the group of people they represent has to have made significant contributions.)

I have seen lack of action completely sabotage important corporate projects. This occurs when the senior management are less than enthusiastic about the project at hand and although they give their approval for it, simply do not back that up with any sort of enthusiasm or belief. I always make it clear that senior management not only have to approve a project but they have to be seen to back it up with their enthusiasm, belief and action.

Action is an essential for good management including parenting. Parental messages that are contradicted by their own behavior have negative effects.

Some years ago I attended a conference on teenage smoking. There were many scholarly scientific papers using all manner of sophisticated analysis. The last presentation of the day was given by Mark Keller[10] Mark's first words were the clearest and most succinct of the day.

"Children smoke because their parents do," he announced.

It's true. When both parents smoke a child has an 80% chance of being a smoker. The statistic is similar for other behaviors. Parental actions is, therefore, the biggest communicator of values.

---

[10] Mark Keller was a self taught man who held various positions at Rutgers University and was influential in the world of addictions

Making Drug Prescription More Potent

How can physicians, prescribers and pharmacists make a drug more potent without changing the dosage or the chemical ingredients? For one, they can communicate utmost belief in their prescription when it is dispensed. Consider the following messages and the responses they might evoke.

"This medication has been used for years and it has pretty good success. Try that first and if it doesn't work, we'll think of something else."

"This is a new medication and it's incredibly powerful. Everyone I have prescribed it to reports tremendous relief. It truly is amazing."

All the evidence suggests that patients receiving the second message are more likely to take the prescribed medication and more likely to report and receive relief than if they receive the first message.

The Power of Prozac

When Prozac, a new class of anti-depressants was introduced in the mid-eighties it was almost immediately successful. Why?

The drug itself was actually not significantly more effective than older anti-depressants which too had a high rate of success in diminishing depressive symptoms. It is true that Prozac did produce fewer side effects, not a small consideration.

But Prozac's power was derived from the media attention it got.

First, it was reviewed extensively and glowingly in the media. It even appeared on the cover of Time magazine and was almost universally hailed as wonder drug.

Second, as a reaction to the hype, various groups started to fight against it. Although most of the criticism came from anti medication groups substantially misrepresenting the negative side effects of the drug, the implied message of these opposition groups was that this drug is too powerful!

A testament to the power of this media hype was that Prozac has now claimed its part in the culture. References to it occur in every imaginable cultural outlet.

Patients being prescribed Prozac therefore have enormous cultural confirmation that this indeed is a powerful drug.

The style of prescription message helps set up the client's belief in the product. The style of the message is a function of the prescriber's personality and communication style. Few doctors are trained in communication skills and it is left to their natural style which may or may not be the most effective way of securing compliance and treatment benefits.

Placebo effects are significant. When comparisons are made between the same drugs given with different messages, the more belief, the greater the effect. In studies with analgesics, the placebo effect accounted for as much as 50% of the observed benefits.

What other ways could you secure compliance by manipulating belief in the product or service?[11]

Consider these other examples..

If you were a fitness professional how could you present a new exercise regime to maximize compliance?

If you were a coach of a sports team how could you sell a new strategy so that it would receive maximal compliance by the team members?

---

[11] You could use it yourself and you could provide exceptional warranties and guarantees.

If you were an executive how could you introduce a new organizational system so that it would receive maximal acceptance?

Suggestion supplied in the appendix[i]

Personal Metaphors

The strategy described above uses metaphors from everyday experience. Influence can be significantly enhanced by the use of personal metaphors. Personal metaphors reflect some of the listener's key experiences. As such, these metaphors carry tremendous communicative power. Using personal metaphors is using the language of the listener. Moreover it is using language that is personally meaningful and emotion laden.

For example, I recently counseled a man with extreme anxiety. The cause of this anxiety was a tremendous self consciousness and self criticism. Although rationally he understood that there was no good reason to accept the criticism, he found it difficult to stop and realistically evaluate his thoughts. On the few occasions he could do this, he was able to stop the anxiety because a rational appraisal of his behavior showed that he was a competent, successful person.

As much as I tried to convince him to do so, he found it difficult to regularly embrace the concept of evaluating his negative and anxiety provoking thoughts. Not getting very far with a direct approach, I sought out metaphors that might overcome his obvious resistance to constructive self-evaluation.

Delving deeper into his personal history, I discovered that my client had been a chemical engineer and successful salesperson for a chemical products company. I went down the list of important things to ask in order to understand a person, as outlined in the chapter on listening.

I asked him what his greatest business achievement was. He proudly retold the following story. Can you see how it could be used to help him overcome resistance to proper evaluation of his habitual and negative thoughts?

He explained that when he was a salesperson, the engineering department ordered the termination of the production and sales of one of the company's cleaning products. There had been rumors that the product had some serious by-products that rendered it ineffective.

My client, being a conscientious and enthusiastic salesperson as well as technically qualified, took issue with the management decision to discontinue the cleaner. In fact, he was very angry about the decision because he believed the product to be worthwhile, safe and effective as well as profitable.

He then, single-handedly, designed and ran a series of experimental trials to prove that the product was indeed safe and effective and by so doing, showed that the management response to withdraw the product had been reflexive and unconsidered. His successful effort to save the product was based on careful and rational experimentation and helped defeat the ill considered decision of management.

It didn't take me too long to appreciate the value of this personal metaphor.

"How proud you must have been to champion rational consideration over impulsive and automatic reactions and save the day."

I said nothing more, believing that a running commentary such as "and now you need to apply that rational skill to challenge your own impulsive, reflexive reactions," would make the metaphor too conscious and thus likely to dilute its effect. For whatever reason, the client came at the next session reporting considerable improvement in his anxiety.

The value of using personal metaphors to convey messages is that they carry with them enormous personal energy and emotion. By using existing experiences, powerful emotions associated with them can be injected into the communication.

Here are some exercises to practice the creation of personal metaphors.[ii]

For health professionals:

A client faces an uphill fight against a condition that has just been diagnosed. The client's interests include military history and he was a state boxing champion. How could you use personal metaphors to get compliance with treatment?

For fitness professionals:

You are referred a client who hates to exercise. Their proudest achievements are their doctorate and a successful career in teaching. What personal metaphors could you use to get compliance with an exercise program?

For executives:

You are trying to convince the head of human resources to change a selection procedure that has been in place for ten years. The head of human resources has held several different jobs within the organization, working his way up from the bottom of the corporate ladder and his favorite leisure activity is fishing.

Suggestions supplied in the appendix

Humor

The use of humor is an essential communication tool. Making people laugh achieves several things

1. It creates a positive emotional response
2. It eliminates a negative emotional response. It is not possible to laugh and be angry, sad, frustrated at the same time
3. It increases your likability, a big factor in maximizing influence

Although humor can be powerful it can also backfire if done inappropriately. I was once in a seminar given by an experienced sales and service trainer. He started off with some jokes, one of which involved imitation of a stutterer. He had not bothered to check and thus did not know, that one of the small group of attendees had a speech impediment. The joke put him behind the eight ball for the entire training workshop.

Rules for safe humor when used in groups of two to two thousand.

1. Do not make political or religious jokes
2. Stay politically correct
3. Find out the concerns and issues of the group and make reference to them
4 If you are going to refer to individuals in the group check with them first at it is okay to do so
5 Avoid profane language
6 Be subtle
7 Laugh at yourself. If you remain the center of the joke, you can not offend anyone else.

Most good presenters start with a little humor. It helps relax them and the audience and it helps create a favorable first impression. The initial remarks should not contain lengthy jokes – it takes time to make the audience to feel comfortable to appreciate an in depth joke. A humorous comment or witty line, however, helps set the tone of the presentation and, hopefully, creates a favorable emotional response with the audience. Exactly the same would apply in a one-on-one situation.

Avoid jokes or stories that may have been heard before. Be careful, therefore, of relying on executive speech newsletters for material because such sources are used by others. The last thing you want to do is to create the impression that your presentation simply consists of recycled material.

If at all possible, make the humor about your personal experience. For example, if I am introduced at a formal presentation as coming from Britain, I might start my talk by bridging that part of the introduction.

"It used to be said there are two things with British lecturers. They are inaudible and in America."

This introduction also allows me to check on my audibility!

If you have enough foresight, you can ask the introducer to mention a specific detail about you that you can then use to segue into the talk. For example, I might ask the introducer to say that I have an "international reputation." I can then pick that up in my opening remarks with something like:

"Yes I have an international reputation which means my mother still lives in England and I have friends in Australia."

As much as humor can be helpful in any communication, do not overdo it. Too much humor can dilute the message and distract the audience. Stand up comedy is entertaining but if the audience has come expecting to receive some valuable training, a string of jokes, no matter how funny, will be frustrating.

Humor is not only an ice breaker but it also enhances identification. Laughing together is another example of symmetry - a shared experience that will bring people closer together.

Restructuring

Early on in my career as a clinical psychologist I was working in London treating a variety of anxiety states and phobias. On one occasion, I had three ladies under my care at the same time who were all afraid of riding in elevators.

I decided to take a behavioral approach to their treatment and planned to expose them to riding up and down in elevators until their anxiety subsided. I also took advantage of the fact that there were three of them with the same condition to use the power of the group as a critical part of the therapy.

A suitably tall building with an elevator that went up forty floors was duly chosen and the date set. I arrived in the lobby of the building and, in due course, my three clients showed up all showing obvious signs of resistance and anxiety. I told them that they had nothing to fear. I was going to be with them the whole time and that they would all support each other. I also gave them an inspirational talk about how courageous they were in doing this treatment and this it would cut weeks off the usual treatment time.

When I felt that they had been suitably inspired and were able to actually get into the elevator, I ushered them in to the elevator waiting on the first floor. As I was about to enter, however, there was a terrific crash behind me. I looked round to see that there had been a minor mishap in the lobby, but when I turned back to enter the elevator I found that the doors were almost closed! Before I knew it, the doors had closed and the elevator was on its way to the top of the building!

I am not sure what flashed through my mind first -- the fact that I could not remember actually mailing my malpractice insurance or the details of my client's medical history. In any event, I found myself racing up the stairwell and lunging for the elevator on the sixth floor. Too late! It was already on its way up again. Back to the stairwell and another feverish race to the tenth floor. No elevator there!

Eventually I caught up with the elevator on the fifteenth floor. I waited sweatily but with some relief for the doors to open. The elevator arrived, the doors slowly opened to reveal – no-one. The elevator was completely empty and bereft of any signs of what have might happened to my clinical charges.

Back to the stairwell. Up to the next floor and the next. Then down again. Up and down in ever mounting panic and perspiration!

After about twenty minutes of racing up stairwells, waiting for empty elevators to open, questioning innocent bystanders and generally being in a state of complete panic, I decided that it was time to take stock of the situation and devise a rational plan for finding the three clients that I had lost. After all, this was a new experience – I had never lost one client before let alone three at the same time.

I struggled into the cafeteria located on the third floor, deep in anxious thought about what to do next. You can imagine my surprise, therefore, when I heard a cheery voice cry out from a nearby table. Yes, you can guess who was sitting there.

Contrary to my worst expectations, my three clients were not nervous wrecks on the brink of breakdown. No, I was the one in that state. They, on the contrary, seemed relaxed and cheerful. The irony of this reversal of roles was not lost at all on my three clients.

"You need to sit down, Dr. Rankin," one of them said, adding "You don't look very well at all," a statement that they all seemed to find more than a little amusing.

"What happened to you?" I asked, relief replacing panic as my predominant feeling.

"We got into the elevator and watched you turn when you heard that crash. Then the elevator doors began to close. You should have seen your face when you realized you weren't going to make it into the elevator. We started laughing so hard that none of us thought to open the doors."

In fact, these women laughed so hard, they did not stop until they got to the thirtieth floor.

If you are roaring with laughter, you can not be feeling any anxiety. For the first time, these women experienced riding an elevator without feeling any anxiety! Moreover, they were more concerned about me not getting into the elevator rather than them getting out of it!

Clearly, there was benefit in the fact that there were three clients and that they could all support each other. And, no doubt, once one of them started laughing it was easier for the others to catch the humor in the situation. I do not know what would have happened if there had only been one client. My suspicion is that single client would have been highly traumatized by the situation and not found it amusing it all. As it was, these three women were able to significantly *restructure* their experience of riding in elevators. I used this opportunity to get them riding up and down in the elevator, together and on their own, and found that the unplanned incident had resulted in significant reduction in anxiety and ability to use the elevator in all three women.

I would like to be able to claim that I had planned the whole scenario as a brilliant and creative therapeutic maneuver. The fact is that I cannot claim any such thing. I just got lucky.

The important principle that was demonstrated to me that day has stayed with me ever since. You can change perception significantly, and thus subsequent behavior, by restructuring a person's experience and perception. Perception is reality.

Milt Erickson was a master at restructuring client's experiences. For example, it would not be uncommon for him to get his clients to jog on the spot for a few minutes so that they would attribute their heightened physiological arousal to physical exercise rather then psychological discomfort of the therapy session!

Our experiences and perception undergo this sort of restructuring, or reframing, all the time. An interaction with a friend makes you angry and suddenly your pal is seen in a completely different light. An activity that you enjoy becomes boring and you lose interest in it. The person you were falling in love with really upsets you and all the warm fuzzy romantic feelings you had about them disappear. We change our minds as a result of new information and different experiences. Restructuring is a natural phenomenon. The expert communicator learns how to restructure the experience of his listener so that they are more receptive.

A Reframing Exercise

In my career, I have met many clients who labeled themselves as the proverbial square peg in a round hole. This is almost always a function of being raised in a family which made them feel the odd man out. These clients feel as if they are the misfits – the victims and scapegoats – of family life. This label, which soon becomes internalized by the developing child within such a family, is incredibly adhesive and will stick with someone in almost any situation including the work setting.

Logically it can be understood that we can not chose our family. We share genetic material with our parents but we might not share anything else. The value system created by the family may not be ours. It's possible to be in a family and feel that you do not belong. This is not an uncommon occurrence.

Just because you do not fit into your family, however, does not mean that you cannot fit into any family. You might have groups of friends and other social networks into which you fit just fine. The problem is one of definition. You have to define who you are separately from your family of origin. And the origin is merely a point at which you start, not where you end up or have to remain.

So to all of those who label themselves as misfits I simply ask, "Do you want to remain an ugly duckling or discover that you are a beautiful swan?"

Restructuring
I love watching my 8 year old son playing with his Lego. He can construct wonderful models then pull all the bits apart and make something completely different from exactly the same pieces.

Visual metaphors

A visual metaphor entails performing an action that represents the abstract idea that you are trying to convey.

Visual metaphors are particularly useful because they depend on the sense of sight rather than hearing, which words do. They also contain an element of surprise and grab the audience's attention. Every good presentation I have ever witnessed employed at least one good visual metaphor.

Here are some examples that I have seen and some that I have created.

<u>Concept;</u>	The importance of being focused
<u>Visual metaphor:</u>	Blurring the image on the overhead
<u>Concept:</u>	Don't fill your schedule so that you're on overload
<u>Visual metaphor:</u>	Filling a glass of water until it overflows and makes a mess
<u>Concept:</u>	Overcome imposed limitations
<u>Visual metaphor:</u>	Breaking a mold or a container that limits the growth of its contents
<u>Concept:</u>	Getting a different perspective
<u>Visual metaphor:</u>	Standing on a table

Visual demonstrations are different from visual metaphors in that they actually demonstrate the point in question rather than represent it. These, too, have the advantage of being visual and thus easier to understand and their images are much more lasting and memorable.

A picture is worth a thousand words

For example, one of the best demonstrations I have ever witnessed concerned the number of fat grams in certain foods. The information was provided in numerical form first. The

98

demonstrator told his audience that there were X grams of fat in this food, Y grams of fat in that food, and so on. He then demonstrated the fat content of foods by actually spooning out the number of fat grams in each food. Watching the grease accumulate was not only illustrative of amount, it provided a visual image that acted as a powerful deterrent.

Here are some exercises in the creation of visual metaphors

For health professionals:
A client requires spinal fusion surgery. What visual demonstration and/or visual metaphor could be used to describe the procedure in a favorable way?

For salespeople:
You want to demonstrate the enormous savings a client can make purchasing your product. How could that be visually demonstrated using something more than a diagram or graphic representation?

For executives:
You want to demonstrate the relative performance of different teams of shift workers to encourage group spirit and some healthy competition. What visual demonstrations could you use?

[iii]Suggestions supplied in the appendix

Perceptual Contrast
We live in a state of constant flux. Physiologically and psychologically we prefer a state of balance. We don't want to experience wild swings in our experience. Indeed our bodies are designed to prevent such wild fluctuations through the process of homeostasis literally, the "same level."

Homeostatic mechanisms operate constantly, often without our knowledge. When we eat, insulin is released to counteract the rise in blood-glucose level. When we go into the light our pupils contract to minimize the amount of light entering our eye. We consume substances that increase our arousal and our bodies naturally relax to counteract the effect of this arousal.[12]

Any sudden change in our physical and psychological environment is not only noticed but exaggerated in importance. This exaggeration is necessary for survival. We need to pay extra special attention to dramatic changes that potentially signal a significant threat.

One effect of this heightened reaction to sudden change is a phenomena called "perceptual contrast." Simply stated the principle implies that reaction to a message will depend on it's *position relative to expectations.*

This tactic is well known to every underachieving student. To minimize negative reaction to a poor report card the student simply sets up even worse expectations.

"My report is due home tomorrow and I think I'm getting all D's," is a great way of setting up acceptance of the reality of all C's when such a report would otherwise be unacceptable.

We use the principle of perceptual contrast all the time to create the most positive experience possible.

- The good news/bad news tactic is used to moderate the impact of bad news

- A performer prefers to take the stage after a not very good act has preceded him or her.

---

[12] This process is called the "opponent process" and helps explain withdrawal symptoms. Alcohol, for example, reduces nervous system arousal. To counteract this, the body naturally increases arousal. When the effects of the alcohol wear off, and if a big enough dose of alcohol has been consumed, the body is now in a state of over-arousal. This is why symptoms of alcohol withdrawal are symptoms of over-arousal.

Perceptual contrast is important because it can tone down the initially negative emotional response.

Use perceptual contrast to amplify the reaction you are trying to achieve. Either augment a positive or diminish a negative by using perceptual contrast.

Chapter 6

Overcoming Resistance
Nobody wins an argument

Most people are resistant to change. They do not like to give up any control and oppose most attempts to influence them. These fundamentals of human nature mean that resistance will be frequently encountered. This is especially true today where the bombardment of messages from the junk mail world creates cynicism.

Reluctance to accept communications and to change is called resistance. Recognizing the inevitability of resistance and having tools to overcome it are a critical part of being a good communicator.

Resistance is most likely in the following situations:

When we are asked to take action, especially if it requires effort or some other cost

When the message conflicts with behavior or values

When the message comes from unliked sources.

. A solid useful piece of advice will be rejected when it comes from a spouse with whom you are angry but happily accepted when it comes from a friend. A later chapter shows that likability is a powerful source of influence. The experience is the message

Yo-Yo dieting, Yo-Yo commitment

In my role as a weight management professional I have often wondered why some people seemingly abandon a weight loss program when it was going well. I noticed this tendency among married women in particular. I have discovered why this happens in some women. They become overweight and draw the irritation of their spouses who then ask them to lose weight. While recognizing the need to lose weight, some women are resentful about their spouses unwillingness to accept them regardless of their size. Although they recognize their own desires for weight loss (which gets them started on the program often with immediate results), they *feel* (note the power of the primitive brain here!) that losing weight is complying with a spousal request that they resent. Their experience of weight loss is now one of resentment and their continued efforts mean they are doing something that they resent. It is but a short step from there to sabotaging the program altogether. The human capacity to sabotage choices and behavior that are logically sensible is a testament to the relative power of experience and emotion over common sense.

One of the keys to effective communication then is the ability to design messages that do not arouse resistance. Another is the ability to defuse resistance once it occurs. Most of this book is designed to tell you how to communicate without arousing resistance. Once resistance has set in it is difficult to remove it. Inevitably, however, you will confront resistance, on a regular basis. So how is resistance overcome?

Brick Walls and Head Banging

All parents of a two year old will know about resistance. The toddler at this age will not take no for an answer and will continue to persist in his own choices until he or she loses interest or is physically restrained. The child at this age seems to take admonitions to stop as merely a green light to continue the behavior. The terrible twos are thus characterized as a time when the child, for the first time, expresses resistance.

This natural developmental stage occurs when children understand the difference between them and the outside world and realize they have the ability to control their environment. This is liberating to the child who has, heretofore, depended totally on others. Like most new found things, freedom has great novelty value and the toddler revels in it to the frustration of his poor parents, siblings and anyone else who is part of the household.

Fast forward about fourteen years and the same toddler, who was a monster at two but tamed by five, is now sixteen and indulging in the same sort of oppositional and resistant behavior. Curfew times are ignored, pleas for less than ear-splitting volume on the stereo are unheeded and parents have to fight to restore any sort of discipline.

The adolescent is experiencing exactly what the two-year old toddler does – the discovery of new freedoms. These freedoms come from physical, cultural and social development which lead the child to believe – contrary to the views of his or her parents – he or she is ready for adulthood. Any attempt to curtail these freedoms is met with opposition for two reasons. First, they are new and thus highly valued. Secondly, they are challenged and thus highly valued.

The next chapter addresses scarcity and fear of loss as two huge motivators of human behavior. *The more a behavior or possession is challenged, the more it is valued, simply because it has been challenged.*

Watch a toddler playing with toys. He is surrounded by a mound of toys but is paying attention to but one or two. Another toddler comes along and tries to haul away one of the toys in which the toddler has heretofore shown no interest. At the risk of losing the toy, which has not to this point attracted his attention at all, the threatened toy becomes highly valued. The toddler, resisting the temporary removal of his toy, now makes it the focus of his play.

If resistance is about holding on to behaviors and possessions because they are under threat, treating resistance with continued threat would not seem to be a particularly promising tactic. This is precisely what most people do, however.

One of the fundamental communication mistakes is to attempt to confront resistance head-on.

Confrontational techniques typically only increase resistance rather than reducing it. The effective communicator uses subtlety rather than force to overcome listener resistance. It is almost impossible to break down resistance through confrontation unless you have natural and significant authority over the person who is resisting – and even then the chance of real success is questionable. The fact of the matter is, as Dale Carnegie in his excellent book "How to Win Friends and Influence People" says "No-one wins an argument."[13]

Confrontational techniques might occasionally seem to be successful in breaking down resistance and assuring compliance but typically these gains are short-term and illusory. *The only way to get effective compliance is to get the listener to own the message.* No-one is going to own messages that they see as being against their best interests or violently foisted on them.

Rolling Rather Than Butting
If threat increases resistance, it follows that the opposite of threat might be helpful in removing resistance. The opposite of threat is not complete capitulation. Remember, resistance increases when a freedom, behavior or possession is challenged. *Resistance is best overcome by reinforcing the listener's choices, not taking them away.*

---

[13] No-one really wins a war either. In World War I, the allies victory and subsequent demands on the vanquished so destabilized Germany that it sowed the seeds of fascism and the rise of the Nazis. World war II had to be fought to prevent ethnic cleansing but the victors then spent an inordinate amount of time, effort and money reconstructing the defeated Axis powers so they could become valued economic trading partners.

The technique of validating the listener's choice rather than attacking head on is called "rolling with the resistance" and is the most effective way of influencing people to abandon their resistance.

For example, a powerful businessman came to see me to quit smoking. He told me that he had tried everything to quit but has never succeeded in going more than a few days without relapsing. After I listened to his smoking history I asked my first question.

"Why on Earth do you want to quit?"

For the first time in his quit smoking history, the businessman is not put on the defensive. I am not making a judgment of him, nor limiting his choice. Indeed, I am respecting his right to do whatever he wants. Not put on the defensive, he is now free to articulate whatever reasons **he** has for wanting to quit. He surely has some because he has made the appointment to see me.

Using this approach, sometimes called "motivational interviewing"[14] motivation and compliance can be quickly generated. This occurs because the technique of rolling with resistance is not threatening in that it *honors the listener's choices rather than invalidating them.*

In clashes with adolescents, parents often fall into the trap of butting rather than rolling. A teenage girl wants to take an evening job at the local grocery store to finance a new car. She is a junior in high school and her parents think that the five evening a week job is too much. The girl protests and a fight ensues.

The parents begin by saying that they will not allow it. They begin, therefore, by instantly invalidating their daughter's

---

[14] For more details about this approach the reader is referred to the work of two Ph.D psychologists, Bill Miller and Steve Rollnick., specifically the book "Motivational Interviewing" Guilford Press, 1991

right to make her own choices. Not surprisingly, the daughter rebels against the robbery of this new found freedom and is now accused of being disrespectful to her parents. She considers this unfair and that it is her parents that are being disrespectful to her.

The parents now feel compelled to reassert discipline, which means make her daughter feel like a small child. If effective communication is about creating the right emotional response in the listener, the parents have failed.

There is no real need for this scenario. Let's see what happens if instead of butting, the parents indulge in a little rolling.

The first parental reaction should be one of validating their daughter's rights. She has a right to seek out *appropriate* employment and she should be reinforced for taking the initiative. Staying positive, the parents can then ask their daughter what is good about the job. They can then ask what concerns the daughter may have. If they do this in a non threatening way they might well get to hear some of their daughter's own anxieties about the job.

"The hours are too long," or "I have to do it every day," might be concerns that will then allow a discussion of the parent's concerns. The beauty of it is that they will not be discussing their concerns but their daughter's. In other words, she will **own** the concerns.

Of course, the daughter may not see anything inappropriate about the job at all. There are three alternatives for the parents under these circumstances.

One, they can hold off on their concerns, let their daughter take the job and discover whether it really is inappropriate or not.

Two, while acknowledging the daughter's rights, explain why this is not appropriate but encourage her to seek different work within given guidelines.

Three, they can chose not to discuss their concerns head on, but address them indirectly. They might say something like the following:

"That's great, honey. We're thrilled to see you willing to work so hard to get something you want. You know, sometimes you have to sacrifice time with your friends and some of your leisure time to pursue a goal."

Faced with such a response, there is a chance that the daughter might rethink her investment of time in the job and reach the same concerns of her parents on her own.

If the daughter is forced to give up the job against her will she will be resentful and it might interfere with her enthusiasm or choice for another job.

It has to be recognized, of course, that adolescence is the time of resistance par excellence. In the attempt to flee childhood and into adulthood, rejection of parental authority is almost a rite of passage. It is a rite, however, that can be tempered with good parental management which includes subtlety rather than force as a technique of influence. In the end, however, parents do need to retain control. Ideally this control is exerted by getting their adolescent children to develop self-control rather than have it constantly imposed.

Rolling rather than butting requires a leap of faith and courage. By not confronting and trying to circumvent resistance there is a danger that you are colluding with the very behavior you want to change. The reality is, however, the best chance of exerting influence and gaining compliance is ensuring listener ownership of the message. The best chance of achieving this is through subtlety rather than force.

Clearly, not everyone will respond in the desired way. Those that do not, however, are just the people who will not respond to any approach.

Words of Wisdom?

A psychologist colleague tried to use the typical rebellion against parental authority when raising his teenage daughter. He frequently reversed his intention in a tongue-in-cheek way. For example, he would say to her something like, "Whatever you do, don't call us to tell us where you are," or "Whatever you do, make sure you drink plenty of alcohol." Although this little linguistic ploy was abundantly obvious, it seemed to work. The fact that it was delivered in a humorous way and was respectful of his daughter while still communicating the essence of the idea, makes it particularly appealing. For whatever reason, the daughter's adolescence seemed to pass uneventfully enough.

Milton Erickson was one of the greatest psychotherapists to have ever practiced. Although not well-known amongst the general public, Erickson was a charismatic man whose many practices and techniques have been adopted within the helping professions. One of the foundations of Erickson's work was the recognition that resistance (in his case the resistance that he encountered occurred in his psychiatric practice where many are resistant to the very help they seek) could not be confronted but had to be circumvented.

One of my favorite Erickson stories, recounted by Jay Haley in his excellent book on Erickson's work entitled "Uncommon Therapy"[15], concerned a woman in her mid twenties who consulted Erickson because she was frigid.

Erickson learned that the woman had been counseled by her mother that sex was dirty, evil, generally terrible and disgusting. He also learned that the client's mother had died when the client was but twelve years old.

---

[15] Uncommon Therapy, Jay Haley, W.W. Norton & Co., 1993

Faced with such a client, a natural inclination might be to explain that her mother was wrong and clearly had a very neurotic and inappropriate view about sex. Erickson knew, however, that the client would not accept anything negative said about her mother who was idealized because of her untimely death. Erickson recognized that the only way to circumvent the client's resistance was to deliver a message *that preserved, rather than attacked*, the mother and her revered status.

So how can a healthy message about sex be devised that is consistent with the mother's communication that sex is evil?

Here's how Erickson did it – and frankly it demonstrates sheer genius and a complete understanding of how the mind operates.

Erickson started by telling the client that her mother was absolutely right. By so doing he eliminated all client resistance because he was endorsing a message that the client herself believed with all her heart. Yes, said Erickson, sex was dirty, evil and terrible – if you are twelve years old.

Erickson then went on to explain that unfortunately the client's mother did not live long enough to deliver the sixteen year-old, twenty-year-old and twenty-five year old message about sex. If she had survived that long, she would have delivered messages in which sex became more natural, appropriate, healthy and even pleasurable.

Erickson knew that the patient would never criticize her mother by abandoning her tenets on sexual conduct. By making healthier messages about sex completely compatible with the mother, the resistance to change was removed and the client was indeed able to resume a normal sex life freed from the tyranny of her dead mother's own sexual neurosis.

It is noteworthy that Erickson used the client's *natural and strong desire to comply with her mother's wishes to make his own point stronger.* He did this by saying that her mother was robbed of the opportunity of delivering, healthy, age-appropriate messages by her untimely death. Not only did Erickson remove resistance, he actually empowered the message by using the client's natural emotions to convey it!

Few of us can match Erickson's genius for communication. We can, however try to incorporate the principles into our communication practices, even if we cannot spontaneously derive brilliant metaphors and masterful communication strokes. Even Erickson himself had to work long and hard to come up brilliant metaphors and images that are found in his works.

In my clinical practice, I have, from time to time, been able to spontaneously generate these techniques to effect change.

In one case, a woman client had been sexually abused by a family member. Naturally, my client was enraged at the family member and prayed to God to make the abuser sick. As luck would have it, the abuser did become sick with leukemia. Now the client felt tremendous guilt for having brought sickness on a family member.

When my client found out that the family member was sick and had been diagnosed with leukemia, she came to my office in despair and an advanced state of guilt.

Rational conversation and argument could not resolve her guilt.

Slowly, I recapped her argument. That she had prayed to God to make the person in question sick and He had done just that. I then proceeded as follows:

"Well, God has indeed made the family member sick. But I do not think that God would have done this merely because you asked. He obviously has acted this way because you have asked it *and he agrees that this is a just and worthy punishment.*"

I then went on..

"Moreover, this proves what I have been telling you all along. That God agrees with your version of events. That you have been wrongfully abused."

My client had frequently wondered aloud why God had allowed the abuse and had assumed that his inactivity at preventing it was a sign that it was condoned.

It had never occurred to my client that God would not just act merely because action was asked of Him. The whole perceptual shift brought about by this "revelation" resulted in an almost instant change in her mood for the positive. Guilt had been exchanged for vindication.

Obstacles to Compliance

From the Erickson case described above, it is apparent that people will not own any ideas and messages that contradict important values and attitudes. In the case described, the female client would not embrace any message that dishonored the memory of her mother.

To recap, lack of compliance occurs for several reasons.

When the compliant action involves effort or some other cost.

When the compliant action violates underlying beliefs and values.

When the compliant action is inconsistent with current goals

When the compliant action is at odds with the person's view of themselves

When the complaint action requires skills that the person doesn't believe they have

When the compliant action involves feelings of discomfort

When the complaint action results in a negative outcome for the person

To overcome resistance a way needs to be found of making the message consistent with known, strongly held beliefs. This is no different from other communication situations. There are, however, some specific tactics to be sued when dealign with resistance.

Don't challenge. Cornered animals fight rather than submit.

Stress choices. Every behavior is a choice with a price and a payoff. The best we can do is make informed choices. This places the freedom but also the responsibility squarely where it belongs.

Focus on the person's goals. Show how the resistance is incompatible with stated goals.

Exercises

For a dentist:
A client has tremendous difficulty in motivating themselves to floss their teeth. What could you say to try to overcome this resistance?

For an executive:
A colleague is resistant in installing new technology in his department. What could you say to try to overcome this resistance?

Suggestions supplied in the appendix

Chapter 7

The Seven Fundamental Motivators
The keys to the kingdom

There are seven fundamental concepts that have been shown repeatedly by social science research to be what motivates human behavior. Knowing these motivators helps in the design of influential messages. It also helps you recognize when these motivators are being *unscrupulously* used against you. With such knowledge, attempts to exploit you can be more capably resisted.

The principles described in this chapter are not tricks or ploys. They represent human nature. Each of the principles reflects behavior that has an adaptive function which is valuable to the individual and society. The principles can be used to sell a car in disrepair or talk someone out of suicidal despair.

When constructing influential messages one should always consider which of these seven motivators are being invoked to elicit action. If more than one of these motivators or even all seven can be used in one message, so much the better.

The seven fundamental motivators are: Consistency, commitment, reciprocity, social proof, authority, scarcity and likability.

Consistency

Consistency in attitudes, behavior and beliefs is essential for sanity and survival. Appealing to consistency is, therefore, an effective method of motivation. Inconsistency has to be resolved by a change in attitude, belief or behavior. For example, pointing out the negative health habits to someone who in other areas of their

115

life follows good health practices will create inconsistency that will need to be resolved.

Motivation to change is a function of striving for consistency. People change precisely because there is a mismatch between beliefs and behavior which is too great to bear.

Research has shown that addicts often have to reach "rock bottom" before they are motivated to change. Rock bottom is the place at which there is too much of a mismatch between their addiction and the price they are having to pay in their view of themselves. Something has to give and for many, it is their addictive habits that are eventually abandoned.

Moreover, being consistent, makes life easier. People who tell the truth and are thus consistent in their presentations do not have to go the incredible machinations and maneuverings of the dedicated liar who has to continually work at covering tracks, remembering stories and papering over inconsistencies.

The Consistency Principle At Work

Consistency can be invoked in many different ways and settings to encourage compliance and customer or even employee loyalty. Whenever inconsistency of behavior can be shown, tremendous pressure for change and action is created.

I have used appeals to consistency on a number of consulting assignments. One such project involved increasing patient compliance in a large medical practice.

Many patients do not comply with their physician's treatment recommendations. This occurs for several reasons not least of which are poor communication by the physician and misunderstanding by the patient. Against this background, I was contacted by a physician group who were enlightened enough to want to increase its patient's compliance. I prescribed a package of remedies for this particular problem including the provision of simple handouts for various conditions highlighting the necessary treatment action. The physicians were also trained to graciously get

116

the client to verbally repeat the treatment advice they had been given to ensure they had remembered it correctly. This repetition also had the virtue of having the patients make a public commitment to treatment. Commitment is one of the seven fundamental motivators.

Another part of the package focused on the consistency principle and addressed the *in*consistency of seeking medical help and then not following through with it. Various slogans were created that captured this inconsistency and addressed the need for clients to be consistent with following through on medical advice that they had sought. One slogan was 'Our Opinion Is Worthless - It's Your Action That Counts.' These slogans were displayed around the facility and members of the clinic used them at every opportunity to stress the value of consistency of action.

Many companies improve employee morale and loyalty by making their workplace consistent with the labor force values and behavior. Even if the jobs themselves cannot by definition fall into this category, benefits are offered that are consistent, e.g. fitness centers. The implicit message is "working here is consistent with your values."

Similarly, corporations can keep and develop their customer base by showing that buying their products and services is consistent with the known values of the customer. This is called target marketing.

Consistency comes in many guises. In social psychology it is called cognitive dissonance, in therapy it is called rationalization, in every day language it is called justification. Whatever label you give to it, however, the process by which we convince ourselves that we are acting appropriately and wisely is an essential tool in the communicator's workbench.

We have to rationalize or else admit that our actions are incorrect or, even worse, random. The human mind can be incredibly creative in providing instant justifications for behavior. This creativity is a function of the need for consistency.

The need for consistency also creates ownership. If I have just bought an expensive item, consistency dictates that I have to value it. If I do not, I am faced with the inconsistency of having paid a lot of money for something I do not value. In creating the justification for actions, a bigger and bigger pedestal is built on which to put our choices. These justifications, brought about by the consistency need, are the glue by which we adhere to our decisions. The more justifications we create, the more we are stuck with our choices. It is for this reason that consistency is an important principle in both influence and change.

Suppose you wanted your kids to make a habit of cleaning their rooms. You could simply use authority to impose that demand. For example, you could stand over them with a stick and (metaphorically) beat them if they did not comply with your request. Yes, you would get compliance but it would be limited. The net effect of this tactic would be to get compliance while you were there and the threat was present. When and if the threat was removed, compliance would likely disappear. This is impractical because you are not going to spend a significant part of your life standing over your kids as they clean their rooms.

Even if your kids complied when you were not there out of fear of punishment on your return, the chances are that you are teaching them to hate the task of cleaning their room and developing a lifelong resistance to the behavior. Motivation is about creating a positive emotional response.

Instead of using force and threats, appeal to the child's need for consistency. Is there a way you can make cleaning the room consistent with the child's values? Keeping a room tidy could be compatible with the following values.

- Being in control

- Having self discipline

- Pleasing parents

Compliance can be achieved if it can be shown that cleaning a room is compatible with the child's values. Then, get the child to commit to room cleaning publicly. Draw up a short contract outlining the duties to be performed and have the child sign it.

In discussing this with your children, keep focused on the positive. Focus on the rewards of doing the task and the meaning doing it well will have. Find ways to make the chore enjoyable. You can make almost any behavior a habit if you associate it with enjoyable feelings. How can you make cleaning a room enjoyable?

- Play your favorite music while doing it

- Make it an exercise regime by doing it fast

- Have friends help

Commitment

Public commitment increases the probability of action. That is why it is generally helpful to get others to sign contracts or make public statements that crystallize their commitment to a course of action. In the case of the medical practice described earlier, patients were asked to repeat to the physician the prescribed course of action so that commitment would be enhanced.

Rather than forcing the adoption of a behavior or attitude, it needs to grow on its own. In other words, one goal is to create ownership of ideas and actions.

Ownership is the currency of influence

The goal of purposive communication is to get the audience to own the idea you are trying to convey. Sometimes, however, egos get in the way of this fundamental principle. Purposive communication gets derailed when egos are allowed to take charge.

For example, imagine that you come up with a great marketing idea. You mention it to various colleagues and eagerly await the next strategy meeting. At the meeting, the CEO enters and announces he has come up with a new marketing strategy that sounds a lot like yours. Let's face it, it is yours!

The tendency in this situation is to say, "Hey, wait a minute, you've just stolen my idea!" There are situations, especially where significant amounts of money are involved in accurate identification of the creator of an idea, that such a reaction is both justified and necessary. Where such considerations do not apply, however, the smart approach is to say nothing. After all, if the CEO owns the idea it is much more likely to get executed than if he or she does not. I know of several large corporations where there is a tacit understanding by senior management that if a new idea is to be implemented it has to seem as if it is the CEO's.

Force creates resistance. When pressured into action, the feelings of resistance are projected on to the action, which then becomes disowned.

Force is the enemy of ownership

So what is the most effective way of fostering ownership of an idea?

Public commitments are powerful motivators. How we are seen by other people is important. We do not want to appear inconsistent, shallow, hypocritical by violating or simply not carrying out actions we have promised.

Saying something out loud makes that idea or feeling real. Public commitment is like giving birth to the idea, giving life to an idea that had only previously been gestating as a possibility. So it is not just that other people hear our ideas and feelings, *it is that we ourselves hear them.*

Effort is another huge factor in commitment and, ultimately, ownership. If I tell you that you can receive the Rankin Award for Effective Communication by sending $5 and a stamped self addressed envelope to me, you would not consider the award, or what it means, very valuable. If, on the other hand, to receive the Rankin Award for Effective Communication, you have to deliver fifteen public presentations of at least fifteen minutes duration and provide evaluations of each presentation in which 90% of the audience rated you as outstanding, the award and the meaning it has will be far more valuable.

Effort enhances ownership

Effort alone, however, is not sufficient, to completely ensure ownership. For example, suppose as part of a well paying job, you have to do something unenjoyable. Let's suppose you have to visit the neighborhood retirement homes and talk to the aged and infirm. The values that this activity has for you is mitigated by the fact that you are getting paid handsomely to do it. You might derive some benefit from it, but the chances are that the experience will allow you to simply label yourself as a loyal employee.

Now suppose that you have a child in the Boy Scouts or Girl Guides. Their Christmas exercise is to tour the neighborhood retirement homes and talk to the aged and infirm. As a supporter of your child's activities you willingly accompany him or her on the trip, taking time to talk to the aged and the infirm. The result of this exercise is that you are likely to see yourself as a public spirited citizen who prides themselves on their altruism. You are much more likely to value the experience -- and you -- because *you chose to do it rather than were given a large incentive to do so.*

Studies have reinforced this fundamental notion. If a big incentive is given to perform an action, that action will not be as valued as much as when no incentive is received. When actions are dictated by money, the task itself does not have to be rationalized as meaningful or valuable. The reward, often money, is the justification.

Herein lies a major problem with a society of individuals who only act if there is a big enough incentive. The incentive itself, becomes the only thing that matters and the only thing of value.

If there is no or little incentive, the person has to come up with the justification for the effort they expend. The likeliest justification they will come up with is that the task itself was valuable enough to deserve such effort. Once that connection is made, and that a task or behavior is seen as valuable, ownership occurs.

Getting Children to Adopt Important Values

If you want your children to value certain behaviors, like hygiene, organization, tidiness, they have to be taught to value these traits. If they are bribed to do these actions with big financial incentives, they will not value the task, only the incentive they get from it. Moreover, they will never get in the habit of valuing behaviors for their intrinsic value. Instead, they will only ever see the important life skills and traits as a means to extort money from you.

In order to teach behaviors in a way that will be valued do the following.

- Spell out the relationship between the task and the broader concept. Articulate the deeper meaning of the behavior. For example, when getting your children to floss their teeth, explain how this behavior relates to the broader concept of taking care of themselves and their body.

- Small incentives can be given to get the task *initiated*. Make the task require effort. Remember, if no effort is required the task will not be valued. Reinforce the child on completion of the activity.

- The whole process will, however, be completely undermined if you as parents, do not practice what you preach. Even if you utilize all the tools of influence just described, if you are seen as hypocritical the wrong associations and emotions will accompany the task and nothing will be learned. The experience is the message.

We have to justify our behavior to maintain consistency and sanity. If we have expended effort on any activity without a significant reward for doing so, we have to justify our effort by valuing the behavior and the meaning it represents.

Once we have made an investment, whether that is in time, effort or choice, we then seek ways to convince ourselves that this was the right thing to do. If, for example, you are seeking to buy a new car and ultimately make a choice, that choice will be justified in a number of ways. Positive comments about the chosen car and negative comments about the cars not chosen, will be sought. Time will be spent looking in the brochure at all the positive features of your choice. You will notice how good your choice of car looks when it is on the road while observing the flaws and disadvantages of other cars. In short, you will really own the choice.

Salespeople know how cognitive dissonance works. Unscrupulous salespeople will use the process of ownership to actually get commitment to their product and price. The technique of low-balling is well described in Robert Cialdini's excellent book Influence: Science and Practice[16]

"For certain customers, a very good price, perhaps as much as $400 below competitor's price is offered on a car. The good deal, however, is not genuine: the dealer never intends it to go through. Its only purpose is to cause prospects to *decide* to buy one of the dealership's cars. Once he decision is made, a number of activities develop the customer's sense of personal commitment to the car – a fistful of purchase forms are filled out, extensive financing terms are arranged, sometimes the customer is encouraged to drive the car for a day before signing the contract, 'so you can get the feel of it and

---

[16] Influence: Science and Practice, Harper Collins College Publishers, 1993

show it around the neighborhood and at work." During this time, the dealer knows, customers typically develop a range of new reasons to support their choice and to justify the investments they have now made.

Then something happens. Occasionally an "error' in the calculations is discovered – maybe the salesperson forget to add the cost of the air conditioner, and if the buyer still requires air conditioning, $400 must be added to the price. To throw suspicion off themselves, some dealers let the bank handling the financing find the mistake. At other times, the deal is disallowed at the last moment; the salesperson checks with his or her boss, who cancels it because "the dealership would be losing money." For only another $400 the car can be had, which in the context of a multi-thousand dollar deal, doesn't seem too steep, as the salesperson emphasizes, the cost is equal to competitors' and "This is the car you chose, right?"

No matter which variety of low-balling is used, the sequence is the same: An advantage is offered that induces a favorable purchase decision. Then, sometime after the decision has been made, but before the bargain is sealed, the original purchase advantage is deftly removed."

Cialdini Influence: Art and Science (p.80)

The Commitment Principle at Work
Making a public endorsement of a product or service enhances commitment. Employee loyalty could be encouraged by making each person publicly pledge allegiance to the company on a daily basis. This would probably seem too much like staged propaganda and not be effective but there are other more subtle ways of achieving commitment through public actions.

Wearing a uniform is one way of showing commitment. Clothing is part of public identity and will thus enhance commitment to the message that the clothing conveys. After all, nobody would walk around wearing a T-shirt heralding the name of the sports team that they hated the most. Clothes, and the messages on them, make a statement about the wearer's identity and beliefs.

This was brought home to me recently when I was attempting some freelance creativity for Tim Doughtie and my other friends at High Cotton Inc. This successful company peddles creative and funny gift items: T-shirts, doormats, aprons, etc. After what I imagined to be a particularly creative session, I presented the executive team with all manner of clever and witty sayings for possible T-shirt design. They were all rejected because, while mildly witty, none of the designs expressed messages that people would identify with or want to commit to. Even T-shirts, especially T-shirts, make statements that their owners want to endorse. General concepts, no matter how clever, just do not make it.

So both employee and customer loyalty can be enhanced by providing clothes that, when worn, enhance the wearer's commitment to the company.

Another way that corporations attempt to enhance customer commitment is through competitions. Here, there is a marked difference between the European and American way of exploiting the commitment compliance tool.

In my native Britain, competitions run by corporations require the entrant to make up a clever phrase or saying about the company or its products. In America, all entrants have to do is simply write "I love X's products." This difference in subtlety is part of the culture and reflected in the communication styles of the two continents. Whether the direct or subtle approach is the best way of garnering commitment is debatable.

The more subtle approach requires the entrant to make more effort which has both benefits and disadvantages. On one hand, the greater the effort that an entrant makes, the greater the involvement in the project and thus the stronger the commitment. On the other hand, many potential entrants may simply not bother to participate if it requires too much effort.

In any event, the competition format allows the corporation to get consumers to make a favorable public statement about its products, thus enhancing customer commitment.

The commitment principle can also be an aid in target marketing. Those who have committed themselves to certain principles make a terrific target audience for products that are consistent and relevant to those principles. For example, people signing a petition about road safety would be good targets for those selling the safest cars. People who subscribe to magazines about the environment would be good targets for those selling recycling or other ecologically sensitive products.

Reciprocity

A fundamental rule of human behavior is that if you do something for me I will want, or at the very least feel obligated, to return the favor. Such reciprocity drives an enormous amount of human interaction, from the bedroom to the boardroom.

Anthropologists and sociologists have determined that the reciprocal rule is a specifically human attribute. The rule is fundamental in the development of a mutually dependent society. The reciprocal rule, in which one person will feel obligated to return a favor, allows for one person to offer to share or provide resources without feeling that they are being given away and thus lost. In short, the reciprocity rule allows for people to initiate a mutual exchange of resources. Without these rules in place, few would want to initiate such interaction and society would be reduced to a collection of individuals left to fend for themselves.

The reciprocity rule is so important to the effective functioning of society that all of us have been well-trained to accept and preserve this principle.

Of course, the rule has been exploited by marketers in many different ways, from the free sample to the dinner voucher offered by time share salespeople.

126

The obligation engendered by reciprocity will feel so strong that it will override other factors that normally influence your behavior. For example, studies have shown that the reciprocity rule works whether you like the person you feel obligated to *or whether you do not.*

Friendship and closeness actually moderate the reciprocity rule. In a close relationship, close tabs can not be kept on every single giving act. In these close relationships, therefore, reciprocity works in a more general way. We might reciprocate tit for tat on every interaction with our spouses but it is more likely that we will work to ensure that *overall* the relationship is mutually reciprocal and fair. When one party feels that a close relationship is not fair in its sharing of resources, problems arise. The perception of unfair power sharing is one of the most common problems presented by couples in counseling.

The problem with reciprocity is one of degree. I might do a small favor for you and then expect a large one in return. This is one reason why people with wealth or power are very reticent for others to do them favors. The reciprocal expectation may be too unreasonable.

Not only is the reciprocity rule extraordinarily powerful, it applies even when the initial favor is uninvited. Marketers have found, for example, that by providing free samples of products to *anyone,* their subsequent sales pitch is three times more successful.

The fact that reciprocity works on uninvited favors has another important implication. It gives power to the person initiating the reciprocity process. If I hand you a $1 bill, I may have given you a small amount of money but I have also bought your obligation.

Reciprocity was a tactic used some years ago by the author of an amusing set of books published under the title of "The Letters of Henry Root." The author, a British satirist, wrote amusing letters to people in public life in the hopes of publishing their responses. No doubt, if he just wrote the letters and sat back waiting for the replies to come flooding in, he would have been mightily disappointed. However, he invoked the reciprocity rule. With every letter he enclosed a one-pound note (about $1.50). This made a reply significantly more likely.

The author also invoked the reciprocity rule in another way. In the first volume of letters, he published his initial letter with the enclosed money and simply stamped a large NO REPLY! across the letter when the recipients failed to respond to the reciprocity rule. This significantly increased the replies he got for his subsequent books. Why? Because nobody, least of all those in the public eye with a reputation to consider, want to publicly be seen violating the reciprocity rule. Most of us will go out of our way not to be viewed as users, leeches and ingrates. So for the cost of less than two dollars the author was able to get replies to letters that might normally be simply dispensed to the trash compactor.

Reciprocity is the engine of social exchange

The reciprocity rule can be exploited, and frequently is. Confidence tricksters will use reciprocity to gain their victim's compliance. In order to off-load the discomfort of obligation we will sometimes agree to a course of action that is disproportionate to the normal dictates of the reciprocity rule. The con artist will also stimulate feelings of obligation and then extract a favor which is far larger than warranted by the initial favor.

The reciprocity principle is implicated in several types of clinical problems and personality disorders, some of which could be characterized as 'reciprocity disorders'. Some people have an overdeveloped sensitivity to the reciprocity rule and seem to feel perpetually obligated to everyone, often with disastrous consequences. Such people are often described as co-dependent. At the other end of the scale are those who seem to have no sensitivity to the rule and feel no obligation at all. These are isolated people with serious deficiencies in social interaction. Then, there are those who have been trained at an early age to exploit the reciprocity rule – the con artists and the manipulators. Individuals who have had their trust violated often have problems with reciprocity and dislike having others acting kindly towards them either because they are suspicious of the motivation involved and/or because they do not want to feel obligated in any way.

Research has also revealed another important dimension of reciprocity. A technique called rejection-then-retreat involves a request for a favor which when rejected is followed by a request for a smaller favor. *The reduction in the request is seen as a concession, and thus invokes the reciprocity rule.* This happens even if the initial request was uninvited!

I encounter examples of this approach all the time. Here's a typical scenario.

My phone rings and I answer it.

Caller: Is this Dr. Rankin?

Me: Yes, who is this?

Caller: Dr Rankin, how are you today?

Me: Busy. Can you get to the point.

Caller: I'm calling today on behalf of the sick animals of blind, handicapped children of disabled, decorated veterans of South Carolina. Dr. Rankin, our organization provides much needed support for this group Your contribution of $35 will allow..

Me: What's the smallest contribution I can make?

Caller: $15

Me: Send me the pledge form for $15

Caller: Thank you so much, Dr. Rankin. I would just like to...

Me: That's okay. Glad to help. Goodbye.

Clearly the caller is an experienced solicitor and I am an experienced sucker. First, he not only asked an initial favor but did not make it so unreasonable that I would immediately hang up. It is possible that I will buy the $35 deal but when I do not he can always come back with a smaller request. In fact, I have been so trained to accept this technique that I make the request for him!! Obviously the "smallest contribution I can make" is absolutely nothing but reciprocity forces me, at least on this occasion, to comply with the request.

The beautiful thing about the rejection-then-retreat technique is that overall, people like me who fall for it, feel that it is a satisfactory arrangement and they own the deal. This is important because it means a) I am likely to actually send in the money I pledged and b) I will be willing to entertain similar requests in the future. By making me feel that I have negotiated the deal, the clever communicator makes me feel as if I have had some control over the bargaining process.

Of course, there are days when I have been reciprocity-ed to death and am in no mood for further insults to my sense of obligation.

Caller: Is this Dr. Rankin?

Me: Yes, who is this?

Caller: Dr Rankin, how are you today?

Me: Busy. Can you get to the point.

Caller: I'm calling today on behalf of sick animals of the blind, handicapped children of disabled, decorated veterans of South Carolina. Dr. Rankin our organization provides much needed support for this group Your contribution of $35 will allow..

Me: Just wait a minute. Is your organization a 501c3 registered charity?

Caller: Yes, Dr Rankin it is.

Me; Can you tell me your federal identification number?

Caller: We don't normally give that information out Dr Rankin.

Me: Well, perhaps you can tell me what your annual revenue is and what percentage goes to administrative purposes?

Caller: I don't have that information to hand right now, sir.

Me: How exactly will my contribution, if I make a contribution, be spent?

Caller: It will go to a very good cause sir.

Me: Can you fax or send me information about your organization?

Caller. No, sir. We don't have any.

Me: Well, I'm so glad you called. In fact, I was about to call you. I wonder whether you would be interested in contributing to the Distressed Families of Abused Psychologists. For a contribution of a mere $15... Hello. Hello. Are you still there?

Cynicism abounds to the overuse of the reciprocity rule by marketers and con men. So much cynicism that there is a serious erosion of this fundamental principle of social interaction. We are so bombarded with the constant abuse of our sense of obligation that there is a real danger that we will simply become paranoid of any attempt to invoke it and thus lose our sense of obligation altogether. Indeed, there are strong signs in contemporary society that such sense of obligation has already worn dangerously thin. Bankruptcies are almost the norm. Contracts seem to be worthless.

Most social interactions are governed by a what's-in-it-for-me mentality – an attitude that has, no doubt, been fostered by constant abuse of our innate obligation.

One of the main reasons I do not offer an initial free consultation in my psychology practice (as many professionals do) is precisely because of the reciprocity rule. I do not want clients choosing to continue their therapeutic work with me out of a sense of obligation but out of a sense of choice. If it is their choice, they are far more likely to own the therapy and thus find it more useful.

The Reciprocity Principle at Work

The obvious application of the reciprocity rule in business is the provision of various "free" items. These can be in the form of two for one offers, unexpected bonus items that are sent through the mail and special benefits to preferred customers.

The best use of the reciprocity rule is a more subtle application and its one that any business or professional can apply. It's called 'going the extra mile.'

Service in America today is marginal. It is marginal because few people are prepared to go the extra mile to service their customers. At the level of personal one-on-one interaction businesses need to go out of their way, beyond what might be expected, to meet their customers' needs. It is easy to provide a free sample and we all know that it is factored into the company's costs, anyway. So while they are giving us something free, it seems as if it does not really cost them anything to give it.

What is much more impressive than the "free" product giveaway is the spontaneous giving of personal resources like time, effort and attention. So the pharmacist who takes some extra time to explain the prescription and how it is used, the account executive who does that extra piece of research and the telephone operator who spends more time to ensure that you are connected to the right department are all providing something more valuable than the free sample. *They are all gratuitously giving of themselves and in the process invoking the reciprocity principle.*

What most people remember about their interactions with a company is how well they were treated. They will remember the person who went out of their way and the person who did not.

Social Proof

When I was in the third grade, we had a class spelling test. The test was self-marking and when the teacher arrived at the last word, which was particularly challenging, she asked how many of the children spelled it a certain way. All but two of the children's hands immediately shot up. There then followed scenes of wild jubilation by the majority who had taken the fact that because the majority of them had spelled the word one way, it must be the right way. The scenes of delight were cut short, however, when the teacher informed the majority that they were wrong. The teacher used the example to make a point. "Just because the majority believe in something, doesn't make it right," she said philosophically.

Well, the majority may not always be right but we infer from the actions of others the appropriateness of our behavior. There is comfort in numbers, and the lesson that morning for the astute social scientist was our behavior and our assumptions about what is right are driven in large part from what we see others doing.

In many situations, especially novel ones, we take our cues for action from what we see others doing. The action of others is our criteria for how to behave and is called social proof. In situations where social proof has been manipulated, people will do all sorts of strange things simply because they follow the actions of others.

In one classic experiment, groups of subjects were shown two lines, one of which was obviously longer than the other. Subjects were asked to say which of the two lines they saw as longer. The experiment had been rigged so that everyone in the group except the true subject all reported the obviously shorter line as being longer. In this situation, many subjects reported that they saw the shorter line as the longer one despite the obvious visual evidence to the contrary.

Social proof is demonstrated in a number of everyday situations. Have you ever found yourself looking up at some unspecified point in the air simply because others are doing so? Have you ever changed your dinner choice when you have heard someone else make their order? The principle of social proof is used when canned laughter is added to comedy soundtracks. Despite the fact that most people including some of the artists themselves hate the idea of canned laughter, evidence shows that we are more likely to find something amusing when is accompanied by the sound of laughter – even when we know that such laughter is fake!

Marketers have used social proof in many forms. The testimonial is particularly common practice and invokes another important aspect of social proof – the more similar the social proof models are, the more powerful they are in inducing copycat behavior. This was demonstrated in an infomercial released a few years ago. The original infomercial was a tremendous production containing the testimonials of no fewer than four American presidents. Despite the high profile of the endorsers, the product did not sell at all. Actually, it was precisely *because* of the high profile of the endorsers that the product – a set of educational books and tapes – did not sell. The average infomercial viewer does not see themselves as the President of the United States. When the infomercial was remade with endorsements from everyday people that looked just like those that stay up all hours of the night watching infomercials – sales soared.

Other ways in which social proof is invoked include the use of statistics. A product is pitched along with the statistic that a majority of people prefer the brand in question or that it is recommended by a high percentage of doctors, hospitals or whoever the relevant professional group happens to be.

One aspect of social proof that can be destructive is a principle known as *pluralistic ignorance*. Social proof is more powerful in situations where we are uncertain about the rules that

134

govern that situation. Typically in unusual situations we look to others to see what they are doing. And they are – looking at us to see what we are doing. In short, everyone is looking at everyone else for clues to their behavior. Because we all want to look suave, confident and generally cool, everyone in that situation is the picture of inactivity and the Emperor's New Clothes effect is observed in full force. This phenomena of pluralistic ignorance can explain why groups of passersby will ignore all manner of crimes and mishaps happening before their very eyes. Until the first person jumps in with help, everyone will assume from the inactivity of others, that no help is needed.

The phenomena of pluralistic ignorance can explain some really terrible collective decision-making. Executives at Ford decided against taking action when they knew the Pinto had some serious design flaws. Executives at NASA were inactive in addressing known O ring problems on the ill-fated Space shuttle Challenger, no doubt in part because of the principle of pluralistic ignorance. In group situations, individual responsibility easily dissolves and if no-one initiates group responsibility there will be no responsibility taken whatsoever.

This has implications for the conduct and management of group meetings. Participants should always be reminded that they are responsible for the group decision making and if they dissent from the group decision they should ensure that this is recorded publicly.

Good leaders know how to use the principle of social proof to maximize their influence. Many evangelical shows, including those of Billy Graham that have been extensively studied, arrange for individuals to come forward at precise times to demonstrate their faith. Others then follow suit once these initial converts have shown how to act in this situation.

Major league baseball coaches know, or should, that they do not have to win over all twenty-five players on their roster. If they can win over the two or three team leaders, the rest of the players will follow suit. In similar vein, the phenomenal success of

135

the NBA's Chicago Bulls during the nineties was in no small part due to the fact that coach Phil Jackson recognized that if he could get Michael Jordan to buy into his system, every other player would to.

Social proof also underlies copycat behavior. The shooting at Columbine High school in Littleton, Colorado, occurred during the writing of this book. Since then there have been several other such incidents and there will no doubt be others.

It has long been established that where a suicide is publicized the accident and suicide rate for the area covered by the publicity increases significantly.[17] The accident rate increases because many people who commit suicide do not want their deaths to look like suicides and thus stage accidents instead. How could the principle of social proof influence such behavior?

The answer is surprisingly simple. An angry and frustrated teenager who has not been taught appropriate life skills is so out of control that he has fantasies of blowing up his school and shooting schoolmates and teachers. This fantasy is very scary for him — after all he must be out of control and crazy to think like this. But wait! Someone in Colorado feels the same way and has acted out this fantasy. Perhaps he's not so crazy after all. Other people are feeling the same emotions and have the same ideas. Validation! The feelings are valid and by the very fact that someone else has then and has acted out on them, it must be okay to do so. The troubled teenager has someone with whom they can identify and social proof works its powerful influence.

---

[17] The work of D.P. Phillips has pioneered this line of inquiry and convincingly demonstrated the relationship between publicized suicide and an increase in both suicide and accident rates. Moreover, his work shows that the victims of the publicized suicide determine the demographics of the copycat suicides. If younger deaths are publicized it is younger people who imitate the behavior. One paper in particular addresses teen suicides. It is Phillips, D.P & Cartensen, L.L., (1986) Clustering of teenage suicides after television news stories about suicide. *The New England Journal Of Medicine, 315,* 685-689.

Social proof also goes a long way to explain outbreaks of mass hysteria and even mass hypnosis. In the early days of hypnosis there were many examples of crowds of people gathering for a demonstration and all being hypnotized at the same time! Which raises an interesting question. Are some people more influenced by social proof than others?

The answer to this question must be yes. While social proof is an overriding and powerful determinant of behavior it is clear that there are some – the suggestible and the young – that are more likely to look to social proof for guides to their behavior.

The Social Proof Principle At Work

A common example of social proof in action is the televised pledge drive. Whenever a new pledge is received, a bell rings and the graphic showing the current   number of pledge makers increases. Making visible the evidence that other people are heeding the call to arms is a good way of convincing others that they should be doing the same thing.

Providing tangible evidence of other customers can be done in many ways. It can be done by simply providing statistics of sales - as in MacDonald's "billions served." It can be done by showing other customers making their choices and supporting them with testimonials. It can be done by having a celebrity endorse the product. After all, if it is good enough for Mr or Ms Celebrity (carefully chosen to appeal to the target audience) it must be good enough for the rest of us.

Social proof has applications other than   simply boosting sales. Social proof is about providing models that demonstrate appropriate behavior. So there is a place for good models, be they managers, trainers or executives, working next to employees in every facet of the organization from the factory floor to the telephone room, from the front desk to the back lot.

The principle of social proof also helps to explain why adolescents are so sensitive to peer pressure. Adolescence is a time of social unease precisely because at this stage of life how to act in specific social situations is not known with certainty. Social proof predicts that adolescents would depend a lot on their peers to learn how to act in these situations. Those peers are also unsure of themselves.

Authority

Let me tell you about the experiments of Stanley Milgram at Yale University. If you were a subject in Milgram's experiment you would be brought to the experimental room and told about your role in the experiment. You would be sat down next to a large machine which was a shock box. The shock box had a lever on it that showed mild to severe, almost lethal, shock could be administered.

The researcher would have explained that you are going to respond to another subject in an adjoining room. You would ask some questions and if the other subject got the answer wrong, you would deliver an electric shock. With each incorrect answer, you have to deliver increasingly powerful electric shock.

The experiment begins and as it progresses, much to your chagrin, the other subject does not appear to be very smart. You find yourself delivering greater and greater electric shock. Soon, the recipient of the electric shocks is screaming out in pain, asking for the experiment to be terminated.

If you are like the majority of subjects put in this situation, you turn to the experimenter and ask what to do. The experimenter, naturally wearing a white coat, simply tells you that the experiment must go on.

If you are like 62% of the subjects in this study, you continue to give increasingly powerful electric shocks to another person, whom you have never met, even as they are calling out in pain and pleading for the experiment to be terminated.

When you are informed that in fact no electric shock was given your feelings are not one of anger. You feel relieved.

Milgram's classic experiment has often been cited as evidence of the power of authority. It does demonstrate the power of authority to get people to comply with instructions that contradict their own values.

The study, however, does not show that such forced compliance leads to ownership. It was quite clear that the subjects hated what they were doing and sought any opportunity to stop. When, for example, in a different variation of the research, the victim wanted to continue but the researcher told them to stop, everyone did indeed stop.

The research shows that people will blindly bend to authority and even take actions that are against their will when authority is present. So authority can enforce compliance but not necessarily ownership.

It is conceivable that if you have well organized authoritarian regime that controls the media, people can be persuaded that the regime is right. In chaos, the principle of social proof really kicks in, reinforcing the power of authoritarian models. Once you have started to follow authoritarian commands, the principles of commitment and consistency come into play to reinforce the message and enhance ownership.

Most of us follow the rules but like to believe that we do so on our own terms. Which is why when the speed limit on the interstate is sixty-five, the average speed is seventy-three. We like to push it but only within the rules of the game. As soon as a police car is spotted the traffic slows again to sixty-five.

Bucking authority is difficult but not impossible. It creates discomfort to go out on a limb and challenge the prevailing view or the dominant person.

Let me a tell you about a friend of mine. She is a nurse who recently graduated and found herself immediately placed on the surgical team of a renowned cardiologist. My friend was excited because this was certainly a prestigious job and a terrific opportunity.

At her very first operation, the famed cardiac surgeon asked her to finish sewing up.

My friend was in a dilemma.

"We put twelve sponges in but have only taken eleven out," she said.

"Just sew up," said the surgeon.

"Sir, we put twelve sponges in and have only taken eleven out," the nurse repeated.

"Dammit, nurse. I told you to sew up. Now sew up!" the surgeon said angrily.

"Sir, I can't sew up. We put twelve sponges in and only took eleven out," the nurse persisted.

"For the last time, nurse. I'm in charge here. I told you to sew up. Now sew up!"

"Sir, I can't sew up. We can't account for one sponge."

Whereupon the surgeon moved back his foot to reveal the missing sponge and said, "Nurse, you will do just fine."

The Authority Principle at Work

Authority can be used to get people to act. Once they have acted in a certain way, other principles like commitment and consistency can reinforce the behavior. Authority that is rammed down the throat is likely to create resistance.

The secrets of effective authority are also the secret to good management. Authority is not the same as intimidation. Authority

140

can get compliance without intimidation if the right communication skills and approach are used.

Look authoritative
Dress for the part and exude confidence. Stand up straight and maintain good eye-contact.

Sound authoritative
Be firm. You do not have to yell. Strong figures do not yell – they do not need to.

Expect compliance
Allow the person to feel that they have some control over how their compliance manifests itself. *If they feel that they are complying on their own terms they will own the compliance.*

Once the behavior has been elicited, ensure that other motivators like commitment, consistency and social proof reinforce the behavior.

Of course there are some, who are so suggestible that they will comply with anything and almost anyone. Others will oppose any attempt at control at all costs. So suggestibility is a large factor in personnel selection.

It is easier to resist an adversary than a friend. Psychologically, it becomes difficult to resist someone for whom you have positive feelings. It is far easier to resist an enemy and the more faceless the enemy, the more chance there is to project anger and hate onto them. It is precisely for this reason that abuse perpetrated by parents, grandparents and family members is far worse than anything that could be perpetrated by a stranger or an enemy. The destructive force of family abuse is so great precisely because it is carried out by a person who should love you and whom you should love. It is hardly surprising, therefore, that the most destructive psychological force is such family abuse. It far outweighs the psychological impact of torture carried out by sworn enemies.

> **Likability and authority are an almost irresistible combination**

Scarcity

Some months ago my wife called my office in a state just short of a panic and wondered whether I could do her a great favor. She asked whether I could abandon my professional duties for about an hour and head to a local store to get something important. I wondered what could be so important that she could not get later in the day, but she explained that all of the supplies would be gone within about half an hour. Could I please, therefore, head to the store immediately and wait in line for it to open. There had just been a shipment of Beanie Babies.

Fortunately for her, I was at the beginning of my research on compliance and influence and thought that my jaunt to the store in question could easily be justified as psychological research Thus rationalized, I felt comfortable racing out of my office. After all, I did not want to be last in line.

When I arrived at the store, a line of about thirty people, almost all adults, snaked around the outside of the store. Some were animatedly sharing war stories of their Beanie hunting adventures and others were talking about the hopes for this particular shipment. Yet others were talking about the rising value of their investment as if these small felt toys valued at about $6 each, were gold bars. By the time the store opened, a line of at least fifty had formed.

On entering, there were three salespeople ensuring that the rules of the sale were properly enforced and no altercations occurred in the ensuing race for Beanie possession. Only two Beanies per person were allowed and everyone was to maintain their place in the line. As was the custom, no-one knew, including the store, exactly which Beanies were contained in the shipment. There was some cries of pleasure and disappointment as the Beanie collectors frantically assaulted the baskets of Beanies laid out on display.

142

The Beanie Baby craze is a monument to the principle of scarcity. Distribution is carefully controlled, allowing only limited supplies to a limited number of outlets in an area. Not only are the products limited, but information about them is also restricted and hard to come by. In addition, some of the past products are "retired" making scarcity an ever present possibility for every Beanie and a reality for some. The whole marketing strategy is therefore based on scarcity – of information about the product and of the product itself.

The prospect of losing something or missing out on an opportunity is a powerful motivator. Simply put, the scarcity principle dictates that the less available something is, the more it is valued. Research has shown that this applies to all commodities and resources, including information.

The scarcity principle is a variant of the fundamental economic notion that something worth having is in short supply. Although logic dictates that the reverse is not true – that something in short supply is worth having – our minds simply cannot differentiate the different sides to this simple dictate.

When information has been censored or is in short supply it becomes overvalued. It is one of the reasons why censorship is a double-edged sword. Not only is censored material more highly sought after, it also tends to be more highly valued. In one case, addressed by Cialdini in his book Influence: Science and Practice, officials in Dade county, Florida, banned all cleaners containing phosphates. There were two main effects of the ban. First, residents of Dade county spent inordinate amounts of time, effort and money acquiring the same chemicals from other counties. Not only did they acquire it, many even stockpiled it. These residents did not just seek out the chemicals: they valued the products as superior to their competitors despite no evidence whatsoever.

Creating the impression of scarcity is a standard sales tool. When there is legitimate scarcity, that is one thing, but when it is contrived that is another. Unfortunately, all too often the scarcity is a contrivance.

A good friend of mine recently run foul of the scarcity principle at work when purchasing a new car. She found the car she wanted but it was not in the color she wanted. The salesperson not only told her that the model was the last one they would be getting for a while but the chances of them getting the color she specified were "virtually nonexistent." Reluctantly, my friend agreed to purchase the showroom model. Less than two weeks later she drove past the lot and surprise, surprise, not only were there three more models in the lot, two of them were the color she specified!

I am not sure how she could have avoided this trap. At a practical level she could have agreed to purchase the car with the proviso that if a new model with the desired color arrived at the showroom she would have the right for an immediate exchange. She was, however, in the grip of the scarcity principle where emotions rather than logic dictate actions.

Other contrived scarcity tactics include such well worn favorites of "while stocks last," "limited time offer only" and apparent scarcity of product. In the latter, only a small amount of inventory is actually displayed. When a client inquires about availability, the salesperson none too optimistically agrees to search in the warehouse checking first that this is the item that the customer does want and will purchase. Once the customer has made such a public commitment (to himself as much as to the salesperson) the salesperson retreats to the warehouse and, lo and behold, comes back with one product that for some mysterious reason was lurking on its own.

Limiting the time available to make a decision is also a standard sales and even personal tactic. Here you are made to feel the pressure not because the product is necessarily in short supply but decision time has been limited, often arbitrarily. For example, some infomercials create a false deadline by implying that you only have five minutes to order the advertised product.

Another variation on scarcity is competition. As soon as the element of competition for resources is introduced, all reason is lost. During the sales season, stores are a frenzy of activity as customers battle each other for products they probably do not need and could get at other times of the year for the same price in considered, peace.

Competition is a standard tactic in the real estate industry. To spur a decision a new interested party mysteriously appears, generally with more money, better financing and credentials. You are left with the risk of losing the property and might well end up not only agreeing to purchase but also paying a higher price than you might otherwise have done.

The Scarcity Principle at Work

Making any resource scarce and potentially out of reach, increases its value. The scarcity principle works because we have difficulty letting go. As a result, the scarcity principle occurs at some key moments in life and has potentially a tremendous impact.

In affairs of the heart, for example, how many people marry because they simply cannot let go of a relationship even if it is clear that it is not good material for a marriage? How many times do people stay too long in unhealthy and abusive situations because they simply cannot let go? How many times has another suitor been found when a relationship is stalled at a critical juncture? The newly found competition focuses the other person's attention on the real possibility of loss and stimulates territorial instincts.

The ability to let go is an essential life skill. Change is difficult and keeping the status quo is generally the easiest and less challenging option. Occasionally, people and events make it difficult for us to let go by super charging the scarcity principle and prolonging the agony of giving up a valued psychological object.

Marie is in her mid fifties and three years ago lost her mother with whom she was very close. Unfortunately, her mother's death was the setting for a family feud. Marie could not get any of her mother's possessions nor could she get any of her mother's usual advice and support on how to handle other family members.

Marie was thus deprived of the opportunity of letting go of her mother easily. Grieving her mother now was difficult for two reasons.

First, accepting that her mother was dead meant facing the difficult reality that she was now isolated in the family. Second, without any of her mother's possessions there was no tangible symbolic representation of her mother which would have made letting go easier. Faced with these obstacles, Marie experienced a complicated and prolonged grief period. Letting go had been made far more difficult than it ordinarily is.

Liking

A few months ago, there was a television documentary about a new author who had the good fortune to be signed by a major publishing house determined to invest a considerable sum to promote his work. With the backing of thousands of dollars and a major publishing department, the author did indeed have tremendous success. The documentary showed various stages of this climb to fame from the corporate decision-making and media planning to following him to readings and book signings.

At the book signings the television journalist interviewed various people about their impression of the author and his work. People were buying books up fast but what interested me as an author and as a publisher were the reactions of the general public who were forking over good money to increase the author's wealth.

What I saw and heard was both illuminating and disheartening. Virtually every comment from the book buying public at the signings had nothing to do with the book. They were nearly all about the author. Typical were the comments of two middle-aged ladies, interviewed clutching their signed copies.

"Why did you buy the book?" the television reporter asked. The reply came back loud and clear.

"Because he is cute," the ladies replied almost in unison.

Instantly, one of the problems for the modest sales of my books, had been revealed. Buying a book because the author is cute is like disliking a movie because the concession stand attendant is ugly. The harsh fact, however, is that people were buying books because they liked the author, despite having very little knowledge about him or, as it turns out, the book they were paying hard cash for. For all they knew he could have been a serial killer, but there was something about him that they found appealing and from there it was but a short step to purchase his book. Other comments about him that seemed to predispose the public to him was that he "seemed like a nice guy," "reflected my thinking" and "seems like he would have interesting things to say."

The success of the book was then, at least in part, due to the author's likability rather than just the intrinsic quality of the book itself. Nowhere is this phenomena more obvious than in the book industry where well-known figures and popular cultural icons can command huge advances for books that have marginal literary value, to say the least. Michael Jordan could, for example, probably re-edit his home insurance contract and sell millions of copies because of his popularity. Known figures who are liked have really become a brand that will sell millions of copies of virtually anything simply because they are popular. Which, of course, makes it difficult for the rest of us struggling, unknown authors to compete in the market place.

The simple fact is that likabiliy increases influence. If you are liked you have a far greater chance of being influential. The question then arises whether it is possible to increase the chances of being liked. What determines likability and can you make yourself more likable?

The Determinants of Likability
One of the major determinants of likability is similarity or what social scientists call identification. If the listener can identify with you in some way, the chances of being liked improve

dramatically. Establishing a point of contact is thus critical in influential communications.

The exact nature of the identification does not seem to matter. You may find that you share similar interests, have lived in the same places, like the same foods, support the same ball teams, contribute to the same charities, belong to the same religion, etc. etc. The more meaningful the activity, the greater the value of the identification in determining likability. Rooting for the same baseball clubs could be really powerful if baseball is a passion or only marginally useful if baseball is not important to your listener.

For a long time in my career I labored under the mistaken assumption that to be successful in my literary and public speaking pursuits, I had to provide some new insights and novel approaches to human behavior. This put me in a bind because, just as there are no new sex positions, I am well aware that there is nothing new to say about human nature.

Human nature has been largely understood for many centuries. The Ancients fully understood how human beings worked. How the story of human nature is articulated varies from culture to culture and across time. So I took some solace in recognizing that while there was nothing new I could say about human beings, I could present such material in the metaphors of the culture that would be new. We do not need to learn new rules about human nature, we just need to remember the old ones.

Once I started the process of articulating common truths, I found something quite remarkable. Whenever I introduced a fresh angle on a new subject in my presentations, the audience would be appreciative and interested. When I repeated truths that surely had been obvious to everyone in the audience, their response was ecstatic. Telling people what they already know seemed to be more appreciated than providing something original. I have now come to realize that hearing a so-called expert endorse your own views is comforting. The expert is more likely to be identified with and thus liked and his presentation better received.

So similarity creates identification and enhances likability. Other factors also enhance likability. The author in the example mentioned above was selling books because he was perceived as cute. As much as we may not like to admit it, physical appearance and attraction do enhance likability. There have been a whole host of research studies which show that people rated as physically attractive are also viewed as having many other positive qualities, including intelligence and status.

Eliciting an emotional response is as critical in establishing liking as it is in communication. *People will respond warmly to the people that make them feel good.* This is where humor becomes a huge factor. Get people to laugh and you are well on the way to have them like you.

The goal of many advertising campaigns is to associate the product with feeling good. The good feeling might be sexual (thus the use of attractive, sexy models) or it might be warm and fuzzy or it might just be a good laugh. The actual connection between the product and the feeling is often marginal. Budweiser's amusing series of commercials involving two frogs and a lizard create a warm, positive response. The only connection between these amphibians and beer is that a Budweiser sign just happens to be in the background. The same commercial could be used to sell almost anything.

The Attraction of Humor

In my couples counseling, I always ask what it was that initially attracted the parties to each other. Amongst women, I frequently hear that what they found attractive was their partner's ability to make them laugh. This is also true of men, although seemingly less influential in their choice of mates.

Paying attention to someone also significantly increases their chance of liking you. All of us want attention and few of us get the amount that we desire. Attention is therefore highly valued. Herein lies another tremendous value of listening. Not only do we learn a lot that we can use in fashioning our communication, we endear ourselves at the same time, making it more likely that any messages we do deliver are received favorably.

In the same vein, *flattery enhances likability*. Even if the flattery is considered inaccurate (rather than insincere) the flatterer will still be likable. The salesperson who comments favorably on the potential customer's taste, style, manner or behavior knows what she is doing. Even though we know what she is doing, the flattery still enhances our liking and thus makes it more likely that we will buy. Only in the case of blatant insincerity will flattery fail to have the desired effect.

Flattery and Love

Just how big a role flattery plays in falling in love is hard to say. But flattery certainly signals the beginnings of attraction. Once one partner is flattering the other partner reciprocates and before long there is a positive cascade of mutual flattery that produces highly positive feelings.

Being perceived as open and honest also enhances liking. Honesty makes people feel they are valued and trusted. Revealing feelings and exposing your inner self also inspires trust. When you open up to someone you are making yourself vulnerable and trusting that your emotions will be received in a trustworthy, respectful manner.

The first psychology essay I ever had to write was in my freshman year at the University of Nottingham. The topic was on the ways of reducing inter-group conflict. I learned that inter-group conflict can be reduced by mutual co-operation. The research on this is unequivocal and accords with everyday experience. *Working together towards a mutual goal not only reduces conflict, it enhances liking.*

> ## Extra-Terrestrials to Enhance Co-operation!
> If aliens have indeed made contact with Earth as some have claimed and this knowledge has been suppressed, a great opportunity for world peace has been lost. If the Earth were really threatened by a significant menace, the mutual cooperation that would be necessary between different factions in the world would surely reduce conflict and enhance world harmony.

Liking and Sales

The concept of likability has been used very effectively by marketers and sales professionals. At the simplest level, sales training has included tips on how to enhance likability focusing on the factors mentioned above. So sales trainees are taught how to find ways of identifying with the client, shown how to deliver a positive comment and trained how to engage the client in a mutual co-operative activity. All of these tactics are useful but pale into insignificance compared to one of the most obvious uses of the likability concept.

One approach is to make the sales team more likable, the other is to make likable people the sales team. Not just any likable people, but friends. From Amway to the many different types of multi-level marketers that exist today, network marketing has been shown to be a viable and powerful sales concept. The premise is simple: Get people to capitalize on their likability by selling products to their friends. Regardless of the merits of the multi-level forms of sales organization with which it is often associated, the basic concept of network marketing is as powerful as it is simple.

It is not just multi-level companies that use the principle of network marketing, all corporations utilize the principle to some degree. Business lunches, lavish parties, Christmas gifts and many other friendship gestures are all designed to make the important client, as much a friend as a client. Where these clients are important, many corporations spend significant amounts of money employing people whose sole job is to ensure that friendly relations are maintained with the people who provide significant income.

The Behavioral Components of Liking

The non verbal language that accompanies liking involves the following:

Leaning towards the person but not violating personal space i.e getting within three feet.

Eye-contact generally involves the listener continually looking at the speaker. The speaker uses eye-contact to signal the beginning and the end of their talking.

Smiling. As has been already shown, mirroring can improve rapport. Smiling is infectious and is correlated with warm feelings. Have you ever smiled and been angry at the same time? If you can get someone to smile you are making them feel good, the first priority in establishing liking.

Physical touch can also be important in establishing liking. You have to be careful, however, that you do not violate certain important rules about touching.

There are safe zones for touching that imply friendship. Other zones imply degree of intimacy that is not warranted except amongst your most intimate friendships and still other areas are downright sexual.

The safe areas for light touching in the context of everyday interaction are: elbow and mid-arm, shoulders. Touch should always be light, be momentary rather than lingering. Hugs should be given when there is no question that they will not be misinterpreted.

If in doubt, never touch. In the helping professions, especially counseling, it is a general rule that permission is sought for even a minimal level of contact.

The Liking Principle At Work

Don is a cashier at one of my local supermarkets. Don is the essence of conviviality. He is always smiling. As he is sending the customer's purchases through the bar code machine, he is engaging the customer in pleasant, often humorous conversation. He is always flattering in an amusing rather than a sickening way. He treats you as a long lost friend. He is so well known for his friendliness and positive attitude that Don was even featured in the local paper.

Don is the only reason why I would wait in a longer line at the supermarket, which I have done on several occasions, just so I could visit with him. I am sure there are times that other customers go to Don's supermarket rather than others either because he is there or because he has made them feel good about going there. Don is priceless because he is likable and he is a good cashier.

The single biggest application of the likability principle is simple.

To be successful you have to be likable and hire people who are likable.

Likability may not be sufficient quality for a job but it is necessary. If you hire likable people and train them well, you will be way ahead of the competition.

An exercise involving the seven fundamental motivators.

In my communication workshops, the following exercise always stimulates interest and creativity.

We all know of the fantastic story of Apollo XIII. If you did not live through it, perhaps you have seen the outstanding movie or a documentary about it.

The story itself (and the movie) is a metaphor for coping. But what would have happened if, instead of returning safely to Earth, the three Apollo XIII crew skipped off the atmosphere and out into space never to be seen again?

In this exercise, write the outline of the speech that the NASA chief will give to Congress and the American people in an attempt to get them to continue funding the space program in the face of this disaster. Use as many of the seven fundamental motivators as you can.

Suggestions are given in the appendix.

Chapter 8

Behavioral Tactics
Establishing symmetry

A key principle in human relations is the principle of symmetry. In human nature, the more symmetrical the relationship, the more effective it is.

Communication benefits from symmetry

Symmetry means that two people are sharing certain features. Research has shown that similarity in experiences as well certain behaviors, enhances rapport and communication.

Identification with another person can occur for many reasons. The features that are seen as being shared could be almost anything - people known, places lived, activities enjoyed - but the key feature of these similarities is that the people concerned have shared *similar experiences.*

Knowing that an experience has been shared by another human being is a very powerful force. In many ways, human beings live alone in their own minds and they are always looking for ways to share their experiences. Shared experiences are validated experiences.

It comes as no surprise, therefore, that the most powerful force for change is other people. Group therapy, when conducted appropriately, is phenomenally powerful precisely because group members share experiences and thus become powerful sources of influence.

The thought that another human being has shared similar experiences is empowering precisely because it addresses the fundamental need to feel that we are not alone.

Similarity is therefore an essential component of communication. One of the first tasks of an effective communicator is to establish symmetry with his or her listener. There are many possible points of similarity.

Similar goals. It is critical to establish how your goals are compatible with those of the listener. If it can be shown that the goals are not just similar but actually the same, so much the better. For example, even though the sides in a labor dispute might be light-years apart in their view of terms of a settlement, the mutual goal is to keep the company profitable and allow the workforce to keep their jobs and flourish. Even in an acrimonious divorce, the mutual goal is to resolve the differences and allow each party to move forward as positively as possible with their lives.[18]

One of the first tasks in communication is therefore to show how you and your listener share mutual goals. Cooperation enhances likability and thus influence.

⇒ By listening, you can define the listener's goals in their own terms while providing a bridge of similarity to your own.

⇒ Then focus your listener on the how you are going to mutually reach your similar goals

---

[18] Nowhere is the need to distinguish expressive from purposive communication more evident than in the case of divorce. Of course, divorce is an extremely emotional time and feelings need to be expressed. Where couples are able to take a purposive rather than expressive communication approach to their divorce it almost always works out to everyone's advantage. Being purely expressive and emotional only leads to protracted and unpleasant divorces in which neither party emerges as well as they might if a more purposeful, goal-oriented approach were taken.

156

$\Rightarrow$ Then provide the techniques for reaching those goals, relating this as much as possible to listener's experience.

Similar experiences: Whenever you can reveal that you have had similar experiences, identification with your listener is enhanced. The more relevant the experiences are to the goals of your message, the more powerful the identification but any shared experience will enhance identification and thus communication. For example, an AA group works largely because there can be so much identification. The sessions are typically taken up with stories that enhance identification thus making any later advice more meaningful and more likely to be accepted rather than resisted.

Similar experiences can be found in almost any sphere of life. Places lived, schools attended, people known, teams supported, sports played, etc. etc.

Communication exercise
When talking to someone you do not know well, preferably a stranger, see how long it takes before you find a point of common experience.

Symmetry does not just find resonance in past experiences. The more similar certain actions and physical signs are, the more identification there seems to be. Certain key physical behaviors and signs are so important that they are picked up unconsciously and bring the listener closer. Such behavior is so universal that it has been articulated and forms the basis of techniques for establishing rapport.

These behaviors are vestiges of our preconscious past when instinctual patterns were the main form of communication. The communication dance performed by many sub human species is the precursor of rapport as we understand it now.

> **Birds do it, bees do it, even educated fleas do it...**
> Yes, they all communicate by using instinctive Fixed Action Patterns that trigger programmed motor responses in their communication partner. Even *un*educated fleas do it - the communication behavior is completely programmed genetically, requiring no conscious input. Once you climb the evolutionary scale , these instinctive Fixed Action Patterns, become more flexible, responsive to modification and increasingly influenced by consciousness.

The FAP's of social behavior. There are very distinct patterns of social skills. Eye-contact in normal individuals follows a very specific pattern. When a person begins to speak they look at their listener, look away while talking then re-establish eye-contact before finishing their message.

The physical signs that can form the basis of rapport are:

Similar breathing rates.
Matching moods can also be achieved by matching breathing rates. Rate of breathing can be picked up unconsciously as an indicator of another person's state of relaxation and arousal. Matching relaxation and arousal, therefore, is a legacy of primitive communication patterns.

Breathing can be observed by watching the rise and fall of the chest or shoulders.

Similar voice tone/tempo.
Speech occurs in different dialects, tones and tempos. Have you ever noticed how someone speaking a foreign language seems to be speaking incredibly fast? That's because we are listening to every sound. When listening in our own language we are able to automatically process the sounds so the speech does not seem so fast.

Matching tone and tempo are ways of ensuring symmetry. Regional differences in dialect, tone and tempo can create a difference in today's business environment where companies tend to have clients from all over the country and local operators are talking to customers with different speech patterns.

Most of us are not familiar with our speech tempo and tone. In fact, most of us can barely recognize our voices when heard as others hear us. That's because how we hear our voice is moderated through our own bodies- we are listening to ourselves from the inside.

Communication Exercise
Tape record your voice. Vary your tone and tempo to see what effect it has on how you sound and how you present yourself.

Most accents and dialects elicit associations and thus emotional responses.   My British accent conveys certain associations: intelligence, formality, education. Soon after I had moved to Hilton Head Island, primarily a resort town,   I was in a store where the young clerk remarked on my accent.

"Do you speak like that all the time?" the teenager asked?

"Yes," I replied

"Even on the beach?" she asked incredulously

Obviously the formality implied by my British accent did not belong on such an informal place as the beach.

The other side of this coin suggests that   automatic associations with accents should not be allowed to obstruct perception. The brain's automatic shortcuts can lead you astray. For example, I was recently haggling over an invoice with a company and was eventually referred to the financial controller. When I got through to the controller the man had such a thick western drawl that my image of him was that he had just come in from rounding up the herd! I had to make a conscious effort to ensure that this image did not interfere with my perception of him as a competent professional.

Warning!
Matching another person's voice tone and tempo should always sound natural. Do not try to imitate accents or dialects!

Matching speech tome and tempo will also sound as if you and the listener are in the same emotional place -- reassuring for both parties.

Similar movement
In the early part of my career as a clinical psychologist, I began to notice that some of my clients were copying my movements. If I leaned back, they leaned back. If I put my hands on my head, they put their hands on their head and so on.

In graduate school, no-one formally trained us in the mirroring technique and its relationship to rapport. The mirroring of body posture and movement, however, is a sure sign that two people are sympatico. Now in my therapy, I will use this fact to check on levels of rapport that have been established. In other situations, I will deliberately mirror to establish rapport.

Most of us are unaware of our body posture on a moment-to-moment basis. The effects of subtle mirroring thus occur at a sub conscious level.

Communication Exercise
Practice mirroring in a variety of non significant situations. Try it out with friends and strangers were there is nothing important riding on the outcome of the encounter. See what mirroring works, what does not and whether your partner is even aware of what you are doing.

Similar movement rhythms

It is also possible to match movement rhythms rather than simply mirror movements. Here's how this technique works.

Whenever the person your interacting with makes a movement (touches their hair, pushes back their glasses, etc), you make a movement. Your movement is not a mirroring but simply a small, different movement. For example, when the listener pushes their glasses, you flap your foot. In short, you mark a movement of theirs with one of your own.

Why should matching this way create a feeling of rapport? Who knows? Consider the following, however.

- Pendulum clocks when placed together will gradually synchronize their pendulum swing.

- Women living together will report the synchronization of their menstrual cycles.

Remember that the Fixed Action Patterns of animal communication closely resemble dances of synchronized movement. The world is constructed around the principles of harmony, balance and symmetry. These principles apply in the natural world as well as the metaphysical one. Good communication depends on symmetry and good communication creates symmetry.

Chapter 9

The Power of Suggestion
Bypassing consciousness

I had a friend in high school who developed an interest in seances. It seemed that most nights, homework assignments were exchanged for the ouija board. Each morning my pal would regale his friends with the predictions that had been forecast at the previous night's psychic entertainment.

One day he arrived at school looking very pale. The ouija board had informed him that he was going to die on a Wednesday. Not necessarily a Wednesday any time soon, but some Wednesday, hopefully long into the future.

You might imagine that for a long while this piece of information put a crimp in his Wednesdays. He took extra special precautions on Wednesdays when crossing roads, traveling by car and was generally far more vigilant than he was on other days of the week. On the other days of the week, however, he would take risks with wild abandon, feeling safe in the knowledge that he was going to survive at least until the following Wednesday.

None of his behavior had any logical basis. For one thing, there was no evidence that the prediction was correct. Secondly, even if it were, the Wednesday in question might happen eighty years hence. And even if it were correct, there was no reason to believe there were not as many dangers on other days of the week. Human beings are not logical, however.

The prediction was a classic case of the power of suggestion in action. We are all going to die on one of the days of the week so it is possible – actually a 15% chance - that Wednesday is going to be the day. The logical mind is so taken up with the anxious question of which Wednesday it will be that the message that it will be a Wednesday slips into the unconscious almost unnoticed.

Suggestion works by slipping the message into the unconscious while the conscious mind is absorbed in the details. The first consideration the conscious mind considers in the above example is which Wednesday it will be not whether it might be a Thursday or a Friday instead.

Here's a less morbid example and one in which the power of suggestion was turned into a positive force.

A woman in her mid thirties, suffering from shyness, anxiety and loneliness consulted me. She did not have any boy friends despite a desperate desire to be in a relationship and despite being intelligent, physically attractive and amiable. The problem was that she was crippled by her constant self-analysis. If she even thought about going into situations where she might meet a man she became self-critical, anxious and completely self-sabotaging.

During the course of therapy, I suggested to her through hypnotic language that she was indeed going to start a relationship and moreover this was going to happen on a certain day.

Now, I didn't look into the tea leaves and say something like, "I can see that you will meet the man of your dreams on a Friday." I don't claim to have such psychic powers. I did, almost as an aside, drop the following into the course of our conversation.

"I just read a study in a respected social science journal that showed that a majority of people met their significant others on a Friday."

The conscious mind's initial reaction is to try to work out why that might be the case. Perhaps people are more relaxed at the week-end? There are probably more parties and social events on Fridays than other days of the week, and so on. While the

164

conscious mind is working on the details, the unconscious mind is accepting the message.

I have to admit to knowing no such research. The chances are that the weekends probably do have a higher rate of such significant meetings for obvious reasons. I did have a purpose, however, and it worked.

At an appointment about a month later she arrived to excitedly tell me that she indeed had a wonderful weekend with a new male friend.

"And you were right, Dr Rankin, we did meet on a Friday just like you said I would!"

Actually, the astute reader will realize that I had said no such thing. I never predicted the day she would meet someone. I merely suggested to her unconscious mind that Friday was a good possibility.

How had this come about? My intention in planting this suggestion was to create one day a week when the client thought that there was a real possibility of a meeting and that it was somehow beyond her control. This, I hoped would do two things. It would reduce her self-doubt because she would have a more fatalistic approach to Fridays. There was no point worrying because there was nothing she could do about it. It would also mean that on Fridays she was more positive about the possibility of a meeting and thus go out of her way to be ready for it rather than sabotaging herself. I suspect that on Friday's her appearance, her clothes, her make-up and attitude were substantially changed thus making an encounter much more likely.

Several of the techniques in this book have involved using techniques that work beyond the level of consciousness. These techniques have been designed to make the listener more amenable to communications. There are other techniques which are designed to implant suggestions.

Ericksonian methods have already been described and show how to overcome resistance and restructure experience. Erickson was a great practitioner of hypnosis, redefining the technique to include almost any method that by-passed conscious filters.

Suggestion techniques implant ideas as opposed to simply making the listener receptive to them. Hypnosis is the best known suggestion technique. It is my view that hypnosis cannot make people do anything to which they are violently opposed. It can remove inhibitions to behaviors that otherwise might be enacted and it can help overcome resistance.

Hypnosis

Contrary to popular belief, hypnosis is a tool rather than a specific treatment. As a result, hypnosis can be used to manage any condition but it is not a treatment of choice for any one specific behavior.

An exact definition of hypnosis is actually elusive. Most experts agree that it involves a state of deep relaxation but beyond that, definitions vary. Some people believe that a trance is necessary, others do not. In any event, most agree that hypnosis is a way of manipulating the listener's psyche so that he or she will act in a certain way.

Hypnosis per se should never be used by an untrained person. There are, however, various hypnotic language patterns that can, and are, used in everyday communication.

Hypnotic Language Patterns

One theme throughout this book is that creating the right experience is an essential part of effective communication. Many of us chose not to access our deeper emotions, instead using our conscious defenses to intellectualize our responses to communications. The task of the good communicator is to control the access of these emotions and to be able to elicit the relevant emotions and experiences in the listener that will enhance receptivity to the communicator's messages.

Because of conscious resistance, guiding listeners to these relevant experiences and emotions often has to be done at the unconscious level.

Hypnotic language patterns are ways of guiding the listener to a particular emotion or experience by speaking to the unconscious. They also keep the listener's attention and focus the mind on the experiences and emotions that will carry your message. Types of hypnotic language include the following.

Presupposition

With presupposition, you, the speaker, are assuming that the listener is going to achieve a particular goal or state. This presupposition is slipped into the conversation, subtly and without emphasis. Presuppositions should not be made so outrageous as to be unbelievable. In fact, such usage is a common form of humor.

For example, "When you become King you can do what you want."

The real use of presupposition for influence might be as follows.

"It might take a few days, but before you know it you'll have mastered this technique."

"You might not immediately recognize when you are mastering these communications skills."

"It will be interesting to see the creative ways your unconscious mind generates really effective metaphors."

The subtext message here is clearly the belief that an event is going to happen. While the conscious mind is focusing on the details (when, how etc..) the unconscious is wide open to accept the suggestion that this goal is going to be met. There is no discussion of whether the outcome will happen.

Implication

Implication is another subtle way of suggesting a positive outcome. Again, the conscious mind is distracted by the words and detail while the subtle message becomes received by the unconscious.

"You might not consciously feel more competent about devising effective communications"

"You will not be completely relaxed when presenting effective messages yet."

Experience Focusing

You can imply an emotion or experience by getting the listener to focus on it through a question. This is guiding them to where you want them to be.

"I wonder if you will notice the sense of pride that will accompany your mastery of these skills?"

"Can you notice the sense of excitement as you begin to understand the possibilities of these techniques?"

"Can you remember a time when you felt similarly inspired?"

Conscious/Unconscious Mind Division

By attributing limited capacity to the conscious mind and unlimited ability to the unconscious mind a bind can be created that can really help the listener overcome conscious blocks. This technique is particular helpful when trying to motivate or when in a leadership role.

There is no logical way of disputing that the conscious mind is limited but the unconscious mind is not. Because the power is in the unconscious, it cannot be consciously denied!

"Your conscious mind may be doubting your ability to develop effective metaphors even as your unconscious is busy creating them."

"Your conscious mind is focusing on the logic of what I have told you, while your unconscious is making all the right emotional and experiential connections."

The beauty of this particular language pattern is that most people believe in the conscious/unconscious division and many are fascinated by the power of the unconscious. In fact, a vast majority of our mental life is unconscious. If it were not, and we had conscious access to all our experiences, thoughts, memories all of the time, we would simply be overwhelmed.

Embedded Command
When using stories about others to make a point to your listener you can emphasize the experience of the protagonist in the story to embed a command. This emphasis is made by a voice shift or by other non verbal gestures that highlight the experience in question.

Once, when working with a client whose inability to complete projects was a major problem, I told the following, true, story which readers will recognize as part of an earlier life script of mine.

"When I was a teenager I played rugby for my school. In an important game we were attacking and were about to score when we lost the ball. One of the opposing team picked up the ball and raced away. I ran the length of the field, determined to stop him from scoring. I caught up with him but missed the tackle and he scored. I determined then, **that if I was going to put in all that effort I was going to see the job through.**"

I could use the same story to make an embedded command to somebody whose perfectionism was ruining them.

"When I was a teenager I played rugby for my school. In an important game we were attacking and were about to score when we lost the ball. One of the opposing team picked up the ball and raced away. I ran the length of the field, determined to stop him from scoring. I caught up with him but missed the tackle and he scored. My coach was thrilled with me for the effort, nonetheless, and **I realized I could feel good about myself even if my effort didn't always work out the way I wanted.**"

Quote

Using direct quotations works in a similar way. You can use someone else's words to bypass defensiveness because the meaning is not directly addressed to the listener. So, although the words are heard as part of the story, they are felt as part of the listener's own experience.

For example, suppose you were a physician working with a client who was reluctant to follow a prescribed course of treatment. You might recount the following.

"One of my patients also suffers from a similar condition. His wife was in here, only the other day. She said that she was angry with him for not following treatment properly and told him he was '**slowly killing himself with a combination of selfishness and stubbornness.**'

The quote does allow you to say what you want to the listener without doing so directly.

Suppose you are a corporate executive trying to convince some very conservative and resistant colleagues to change an age-old practice for a new, more efficient one.

You might somewhere along the way slip in this story and quote.

"I was with my neighbors last night having dinner. Their son only ever eats hot dogs for dinner. I asked him why. He said he liked them and knew what to expect and couldn't be bothered to find something new. I said, **you are going miss out on a lot of good experiences if you keep eating the same thing.**[19]

Truism

A truism is a statement of universal truth that cannot be denied and thus enables common ground and symmetry to be established with the listener.

A supervisor who has a subordinate who is struggling with some initial assignments might say the following.

"Who hasn't had the experience of struggling to master an activity only to be able to do it with complete ease within a short time."

A fitness trainer who has a client who is very self-conscious of his/her awkwardness doing a particular exercise might say the following.

"We've all had the experience of feeling self-conscious when we started an activity that was unfamiliar only to get more comfortable after a few sessions."

Bind of Positive Outcomes

In this pattern, two or more positive outcomes are set against each other. The conscious mind is drawn to consider the logic of which outcome will come first allowing the assumption that one of the positive outcomes will indeed happen, to be accepted into the unconscious.

A parent trying to motivate a child to do better at school might say the following.

"I wonder whether you will get an A first in English or in Science?"

---

[19] I use this example because I do, indeed, know someone who only ever eats hot dogs!

A supervisor might say the following to a subordinate who is trying hard to improve their competence.

"I don't know whether it will be the improvement in your effort or performance that your colleagues will notice first."

A leader in a weight control group addressing a new member who has doubts about her ability to start an effective program might say the following.

"I wonder whether it will be the loss of inches or pounds that you will notice first or perhaps they will happen at the same time."

Hypnotic language patterns are powerful techniques. If some of these tactics sound familiar, there are ones that you have used in a simplistic way with children. Children are very suggestible and so these language patterns work particularly well with them. They can, however, be used with anyone with good effect especially in delivering motivational and positive messages.

Chapter 10

Think Positive!
The most important communication is with yourself

Throughout this book the emphasis has been on communicating with other people. The most important conversations you are ever going to have, however, are with yourself.

The power of words to elicit emotions has already been demonstrated. Images have even more power. Imagine, then, the effect that constant negative thoughts and images have on psyches. Negative thoughts generate negative moods.

It is not that negative thoughts and images can be completely banished. Life is stressful and we will face continual challenges. How those challenges are approached, however, is critical.

Some years ago there was a study that showed that depressed people had a realistic outlook – after all there are many things to be depressed about. Having a depressed and worried outlook may be understandable but *it's not very adaptive*. Negative thoughts drain energy and impact performance. The more positive you are, the better you will feel and the better you will perform.

Use the communication tools described in this book to ensure optimal performance. You can do this by...

- Using positive words wherever possible

- Restructuring difficult life situations as challenges and opportunities

- Creating positive stories about your self and your life

- Using and being exposed to humor

- Visualizing success

- Ensuring that you do fun things enough of the time

- Surrounding yourself with positive people. Remember the power of social proof.

Let's try to keep upbeat and challenge negativity wherever it rears its ugly head. Unfortunately, negativity is rife.

Negativity

While writing this book I had to fly across country which necessitated taking three flights the first of which left Savannah, Georgia at 6:00 am. When I got to the security gate there was a long line due to the fact that it was barely 5:00 am and the airport was just opening up for its first flights an hour later. Despite the obvious fact that no-one was in jeopardy of missing their flight, those at the back of line of about thirty were already complaining.

"You'd think they would have opened this before now."

"Now, I have to wait here all day."

"C'mon, I want to get to the gate."

Of course, everyone made their flight. Mine arrived at Atlanta about fifteen minutes ahead of time and as a result the gate was not quite ready to receive the plane, necessitating about a five minute delay in disembarking. Negativity was rife in this situation, too.

"A forty-five minute flight, and an hour to get off."

"Come on I have got a connection to make"

"You think they would come up with a better system."

Notice that even with the delay, passengers disembarked about ten minutes ahead of schedule!

The second leg of the trip was in older plane, a Tri star. The plane was perfectly serviceable and functional, the flight was smooth and arrived on time without incident. By now, I was sensitized to negative comments and couldn't but overhear passenger comments about the wear and tear in the carpet (!) and sundry other negative comments about the state of the plane.

Perhaps it is today's fast-paced life with its impossible expectations, high stress levels and the premium on convenience but we seem to have become an ill-tempered, rude and impatient society. The last thing one wants to do is to arouse these emotions that seem to be just under or on the surface of the average person's psyche, in your communications. That is exactly what we do however.

As luck would have it the next leg of the trip provided the perfect example. The plane was full because another flight over the same route had been canceled. This led to a problem which the flight attendant announced thus:

"I'm very sorry to inform you we don't have enough meals on this flight for everybody. We apologize for this inconvenience."

Oops! Negativity instantly hooked! Mumbling and grumbling from all parts of the packed plane.

There is nothing more infectious than a complaint

But wait! There is a good reason for this problem which the flight attendant went on to explain.

"Because we had a lot of people transfer from the canceled flight we had a choice to make. Either we could leave on time or wait to load more meals. We decided it would be better to leave on time for your convenience."

There's a problem, 'tho. The passengers were already in a grumpy mood and feeling deprived from the first part of the message. And some of them were so voluble in their complaints they didn't even hear the reason for the problem and the reasonable choice that the aircraft personnel made on their behalf.

So a better way of handling this minor public relations crisis would be something like the following.

"Good morning everyone! We have faced a choice this morning. Because of the late influx of passengers from flight X we had to decide between leaving on time or delaying the flight to get more meals on board. We decided that you would prefer to arrive at your destination on time at the possible risk of missing a meal. We hope you agree with this choice."

As a general rule, establish credit with good feelings before delivering messages that are likely to be less well-received. Because most of the time you are delivering messages in rapid succession, the first message has proportionately more effect than subsequent ones. If possible do not pair messages unless a deliberate choice has been made to use a positive communication to reduce the impact of a negative one.

In a good news/ bad news situation deliver the good news first

---

In what would have been leap of communication inspiration that I have hardly ever witnessed, I would have loved to have heard the following.

"So we are a few meals short. I wonder whether we could together make the best of this situation and minimize inconvenience. If you do not want a meal or only want part of it, please let us know so we can distribute the meals efficiently."

This would have, hopefully, had several effects. First, it might have got passengers thinking about whether they really wanted a meal rather than automatically taking it. Second, it might have made the passengers feel that they were pulling together in a cooperative effort and that there was something positive they could do about the situation. *People feel empowered when they have a plan and feel that they can make a difference.* The value of co-operation in enhancing ownership has already been demonstrated.

If indeed that had happened, the flight attendant would finally need to announce the results of this collective effort which I'm sure would have made a significant difference.

"Thank you so much for your efforts. As a result we managed to feed nearly everybody who wanted a meal."

Passengers leave remembering the fact that collective effort resolved a problem rather than the problem itself.

Putting a positive spin in messages it is not about trying to trick people into thinking more positively about a bad situation, even though that is a very adaptive behavior. It is more about focusing their attention on positive aspects of the situation that, in our fast-paced, egocentric society, we have taken for granted.

At the Carolina Wellness Retreat[20] I once faced a difficult situation. An outdoor event had been planned which all of the

---

[20] The Carolina Wellness Retreat is a lifestyle change program that focuses on all aspects of healthy living from nutrition to communication which I started in 1995 and run each year on Hilton Head Island, South Carolina. For information call 1-888-842-7797

participants were eagerly anticipating it. Unfortunately, about half an hour before the event, the heavens opened and there was a torrential downpour making the event untenable. Naturally, there was some disappointment. I addressed the group thus:

"As you can see the hydrological cycle is doing its thing at the moment. And let's not forget the fact that if we didn't have rain we wouldn't have this beautiful planet we call home and none of us would be here. We'll just reschedule the event."

I must admit I was delivering the message somewhat tongue-in-cheek but it received an extraordinary reaction. The group burst into spontaneous applause! Reminding people of the fundamental realities of their existence, which are so often taken for granted, can be powerful.

So stay positive! It will help you reach greater heights and it will also inspire those around you.

Finally, do not forget that all of the techniques in this book apply to communication within yourself as much as communication with other people. Given the power of these techniques, it is more important that you apply them to self-talk as it is with conversations with other people.

The most important conversation you will ever have is with yourself

The tremendous power of words, images and life scripts has been shown. If you are using words and images that elicit negative feelings you are going to feel defeated.

External dialog is a reflection of internal dialog. Negativity and hesitancy in internal communication will inevitably be reflected in communications with others.

So go forward with a positive spirit and know that you have the power to rewrite your life script and make life the best it can be. The biggest rewards in life will come from your relationships. If you can motivate others as well as yourself by making meaningful contact, life will be much richer.

Appendix

From page 81
Some suggestions

Good service is like...a great massage
Good Management is like...air traffic control
Parenting is like...servicing a car without tools in the dark

From page 88
Situation
If you were a fitness professional how could you present a new exercise regime to maximize compliance?

Suggestions
Talk about the success other clients have had with it.
Refer them to clients who have been successful
Provide press clippings etc., that praise the new technique
Provide a rationale that makes the technique unique
Show that you do it yourself

Situation
If you were a coach of a sports team how could you sell a new strategy so that it would receive maximal compliance by the team members?

Suggestions
Show the success that other, preferably high visibility professional, teams have had with the same strategy
Explain the strategy and why it would be beneficial to this team's situation
Provide any material that praises the new technique
Describe personal success with the technique, if applicable

Situation

If you were an executive how could you introduce a new organizational system so that it would receive maximal acceptance?

Suggestions

Describe rationale of plan. Why it is unique and superior
Ensure that you are introducing a new system because of its benefits rather than replacing an old one because of its failures
Provide any collateral information that reports glowingly on the new system
Focus on all of the benefits of the new system
Describe any personal success experienced with it

From page 91
Situation

A client faces an uphill fight against a condition that has just been diagnosed. The client's interests include military history and he was a state boxing champion. How could you use personal metaphors to get compliance with treatment?

Suggestion

Describe the treatment as a battle in which an army fought against the odds to pull off a stunning victory. Get him to remember bouts where he was in trouble but dug deep to use all his personal resources and managed to win.

Situation

You are referred a client who hates to exercise. Their proudest achievements are their doctorate and a successful career in teaching. What personal metaphors could you use to get compliance with an exercise program?

Suggestion

Compare his situation with the struggles he had educating some of his pupils who were resistant to learning. How did he motivate the kids who initially did not see the value of education. How did he feel when he was able to make a difference?

Situation
You are trying to convince the head of human resources to change a selection procedure that has been in place for ten years. The head of human resources has held several different jobs within the organization, working his way up from the bottom of the corporate ladder and his favorite leisure activity is fishing.

Suggestion
Appeal to his appreciation of change that his work experience has shown him and the need to be flexible when trying to locate the right fishing spot.

From page 99
Situation
A client requires spinal fusion surgery. What visual demonstration and/or visual metaphor could be used to describe the procedure in a favorable way?

Suggestion
Use a skeleton to provide a visual demonstration. I've seen these models in doctors practices all the time but have never seen one used as a demonstration! Use two magnets to attract each other to create a forceful union)

Situation
You want to demonstrate the enormous savings a client can make purchasing your product. How could that be visually demonstrated using something more than a diagram or graphic representation?

Suggestion
Construct two models to the scale representing the costs or savings. For example, you could provide the customer with two piggy banks, one 50% bigger than the other, to demonstrate the relative savings.

Situation
You want to demonstrate the relative performance of different teams of shift workers to encourage group spirit and some healthy competition. What visual demonstrations could you use?

Suggestion
You could turn performance statistics into box scores like those pertaining to the favored team sport and update the statistics daily.

From page 114
Situation
A client has tremendous difficulty in motivating themselves to floss their teeth. What could you say to try to overcome this resistance?

Suggestion
"You don't have to floss all your teeth - just the ones you want to keep"
Situation
A colleague is resistant in installing new technology in his department. What could you say to try to overcome this resistance?

Suggestion
I'm confused. Your choice seems incompatible with your vision of leading the most efficient department.

From page 154
Apollo XIII
Commitment
"A great nation doesn't quit in the face of adversity. No, a great people, succeeds in the face of adversity."

Consistency
"In America we are determined, are we not, to be the leaders and pioneers of technological development."

Reciprocity
"Three brave Americans gave their lives for this country, they have a right to expect us to honor their sacrifice by seeing the job through."

Social proof
"The Russians didn't stop when they had mishaps and disasters in their program."

"Other great American institutions programs didn't stop when they ran into obstcales."

Authority
Wear and display as many of the trappings of authority as possible. Be confident and sure.

Scarcity
"If we stop the program now we may never get another chance. This is a defining moment in history and we cannot let destiny slip through our fingers."

Liking
Research what aspects of the disaster resonated with the public and admit to those same feelings to enhance identification. For example, "I, too, share your grief at the loss if these three great patriots."

If there is a very popular (and relevant) figure who can be quoted to support your view, use it.

Howard J. Rankin Ph.D is a clinical psychologist with masters and doctoral degrees from the University of London. A clinical psychologist who has been in private practice for twenty-five years, Dr. Rankin has held academic appointments at the universities of London and Oxford and at the University of South Carolina where he is currently an adjunct professor in the School of Public Health.

Dr Rankin has published over fifty scientific papers on addictions and eating disorders and for ten years was the editor of the scientific journal "Addictive Behaviors." In addition to his scientific writing, he has published many articles in the popular media. He was a regular columnist for the European version of Psychology Today and a variety of British magazines before moving to the United States in 1986.Dr. Rankin has written and developed a tape series *Get Motivated Get Smart Get Slim* and the books 7 *Steps to Wellness* and 10 *Steps to a Great Relationship.*

In his clinical practice, he was the Chief of the Eating Disorders Unit, St.Andrews Hospital, Northampton, as well as consultant to the drug and alcohol treatment units. His private practice focuses on relationships, eating disorders, stress, depression and trauma. Dr. Rankin is the founder and director of the Carolina Wellness Retreat, a lifestyle change program located on Hilton Head Island, South Carolina and The Master Communicators Institute.

Dr. Rankin's work has been quoted in the print media in such papers as The Wall Street Journal, The Los Angeles Times, The Baltimore Sun, The Dallas Morning News, The Cleveland Plain Dealer, Newsday and such magazines as Ladies Home Journal, Health, Mademoiselle, New Woman, Weight Watchers and Prevention. He has been a frequent radio and television guest both here and in his native Britain. His work was featured on 20/20 and on CNN and he has appeared on other talk shows.

The Master Communicators Institute

Founded by Dr Howard J. Rankin, this Institute stages seminars and workshops on all aspects of communication.

The Master Communicator Institute also offers consulting in a variety of business applications including strategic communication, internal communications, leadership and management, personnel selection, training and letter writing.

Using the principles outlined in the book Power Talk: The Art of Effective Communication, the Master Communicators Institute trains people from all walks of life on how to present themselves and their ideas effectively.

For details of how the Master Communicators Institute can help your company grow and for information on upcoming seminars please call 1-888-842-7797.

From Dr. Howard J. Rankin...

7 Steps to Wellness

This book shows you how to control your weight and your life! Most people know what they need to do to lose weight, manage stress and stay in shape, but doing it is another matter. In this book, Dr. Rankin shows the 7 Steps that you need to take for optimal health and performance. Learn how to...

- *Capture motivation - and maintain it*

- *Develop self-management skills*

- *Learn how to develop positive thinking*

- *Develop self-control*

- *Defeat bingeing*

- *Get the support you want.*

Comes with nutrition and exercise guide, 14 day meal plan, daily journal and eating-out guide. Available from bookstores or by calling (803) 842-7797

ISBN 0-9658261-1-2   Price $11.95

From Dr. Howard J. Rankin...

10 Steps to a Great Relationship:
What every couple should know about love

Love is an action not a feeling and in this book, the ten actions that constitute love are described. As well as great insights, the book includes case histories, exercises to assess loving behavior and tips on how to improve your ability to love and your relationships. Discover....

- The dynamics of attraction

- The rules of fighting fair

- The secrets to intimacy

- When and how to practice forgiveness

- How to keep healthily independent and married

- And much more!

$11.95   ISBN# 0-9658261-2-0
Published by StepWise Press. Distributed by Access Publishers Network

Available at bookstore or direct by calling 1-888-842-7797

From Dr. Howard J. Rankin...

Get Motivated Get Smart Get Slim!

This original tape series includes some of the material of *7 Steps to Wellness* on six audiotapes,. Narrated by the author, the tapes include sections on motivation, self-management, mindfulness, bingeing, temptation management, coping and dealing with others. It also includes motivational link exercises and imagery with realistic sounds which really help to reprogram your key associations.

A bonus tape includes "A Personal Message," designed to help you through the day and keep motivation high.

As well as the 14 day menu plan, the nutrition and exercise guides, the Personal healthscope and Dining-out guide come in handy, wallet-size booklets. There are also motivational stickers to keep you focused on your goals!

Get Motivated Get Smart Get Slim is available by calling 803-842-7797

We are on the Internet! Visit us at the following location..

www.findpeace.com

- Newsletter

- Chat room

- Order online

- Information on seminars and workshops

www.findpeace.com

or call 1-888-842-7797